Angela K. Durden

This Little Light of Mine

: Twinkle Revisited

This publication is based on the life and experiences of the author and is considered a memoir.

THIS LITTLE LIGHT OF MINE:
    TWINKLE REVISITED
    BLUE ROOM BOOKS
    DECATUR, GEORGIA
    978-1-950729-03-6

Cover design and interior layout: Angela K. Durden
Editor: Tom Whitfield

Other books by
Angela K. Durden

Eloise Forgets How to Laugh (2004) — Amazon.com

A Mike and His Grandpa Story:
Heroes Need Practice, Too!
(2006, hardback) — www.angeladurden.com
(2012, paperback) — Amazon.com

A Mike and His Grandpa Story:
The Balloon That Would Not Pop!
(2012) — Amazon.com

Opportunity Meets Motivation:
Lessons From Four Women Who Built
Passion Into Their Lives and Careers
(2010)

Men! K.I.S.S. Your Resume and Say Hello to a Better Job
(2013, audio book) — iTunes and Audible.com

Men! K.I.S.S. Your Resume and Say Hello to a Better Job
(2013) — Amazon.com

9 Stupid Things People Do to Mess Up Their Resumes (2000)

Whitfield, Nebraska (2015) (Pen Name: Durden Kell)

First Time For Everything (2018)

Do Not Mistake This Smile (2018)

Dancing at the Waffle House (2018)

Music Business Survival Manual (2018)

Navigating the New Music Business as a DIY and Indie (2015)

Conversations in Hyperreality — and Other Thoughts Umberto Eco and Dave Barry Never Had (2019)

This Little Light of Mine

: Twinkle Revisited

Preface

Since trigger warnings are all the rage in these politically correct times, let's start with one: You are about to become involved with the life of Angela K. Durden.

Think about that before you turn this page.

Because it is next to impossible to reconcile the saddening themes covered (including but not limited to the sexual abuse of a child and unspeakable mental cruelty) with the present sunny version of Angela, a few words of explanation are in order:

Yes, it all happened. There were even worse incidents she chose to leave out. Only a few of her relatives ever read the original *Twinkle – a memoir*; many still do not know it exists. Some people mentioned are rotting in Hell. Others continue to exist in a customized Hell of their making. Keep in mind Angela originally wrote a series of verbal snapshots not to point fingers or wallow in self-pity but to learn from them and move on with her life. Some friends were adamant that she should assemble them into a book; others advised that she leave them buried on her computer forever.

Her life turned out fine.

After missing childhood and enduring a bad marriage, Angela 2.0 understands how her God-given creativity was stifled. It is now in full bloom. She has written more than a dozen books across various genres and runs a publishing company, Blue Room Books, where she coaches writers and designs books (including this one). Her career as a songwriter and live performer has produced her first album.

What follows is a new introduction and the complete and unchanged 2015 text of *Twinkle – a memoir* with a few more pictures. The original afterword has been updated to include Angela addressing questions she has fielded through the years. As the editor, I point out the book is grammatically unusual, written in second-person singular tense. We hope you appreciate the power it brings to the telling.

Read it knowing her energy is boundless, her faith in God rewarded.

Tom Whitfield
January 2020

Introduction

I'm not the first author to believe they wrote one thing only to have the reading public get something totally different out of it or have a reaction the author did not foresee. Most notably I'm thinking of Orson Scott Card's science fiction novel *Ender's Game*. Card was taken by surprise that so many people of different ages and backgrounds wrote to him with similar reactions to that book and suggested they, the reader, needed to know more...and thus the series was born to explain what he thought was a one-off novel.

Just as surprised to hear my readers' reactions, five years later I'm trying to soften the blow of what will follow. Let me state forthwith that I'm happy and steady as she goes. My life is fine. So the story you read has a happy ending. Promise. In 2013 when *Twinkle – a memoir* was written it had no title and wasn't a memoir. It was simply me trying to figure out my life after an emotionally, physically, and spiritually excruciating childhood, and a complicated and long marriage followed by a divorce. It was merely a systematic recitation of events put in chronological order to study —

How did I get *here*?

Why am I here?

Does anybody *care*?

What *value* do I bring by being here?

What made me who I am?

Who am I?

Why did I make the choices I did?

When would I know how my life would play out?

What would I become? And do?

And, more importantly and driving everything, *where* was my Heavenly Father in all this?

The vignettes in the original text were written over a highly intense six weeks and were not meant for public consumption. But then a select few trusted relatives and friends, whom I had asked to read the stories in order to gain their insight, were insistent they needed to be published.

I disagreed, and so they sat on the computer for almost the next two years. Unread. Ignored, studiously. But then, in a thoughtful conversation at a Carrabba's in Macon, Georgia, over a sirloin Marsala, garlic mashed potatoes, and Merlot, Terry Cantwell, a friend who understood my need for a Heavenly

Father's love, challenged my reasons for not publishing. He changed my mind, though it took a whole week before I let him know he had.

After living a childhood impressively full of secrets, it was freeing to simply have the truth out there.

But my focus was always on those events wherein I, upon looking back at my life, could most see God's helping hand; redundant events were deleted. This is my story of my life.

So why were friends and relatives insistent it be published? After all, sexual abuse is not unique to me. It is found in every socio-economic, educational, and religious strata through all times starting with Eve, the first child of God to be tricked and abused by Satan. And thus Satan's methods have not changed. Attack the weakest at their most vulnerable, and hope they turn their back on God, the Creator of all things Good.

Satan wants us to believe the worst when our own hearts condemn us, make us think we are forever unlovable, unsavable, completely unworthy of grace. But our Heavenly Father wants us to know this: "If our hearts condemn us, God is greater than our hearts, and He knows all things." *1 John 3:20*

And so, upon coming to that understanding, I chose to listen to God. He had a path for me to be on — always had! When I finally listened, He gave me solid evidence of where I wasn't supposed to be. My divorce was the first step in seriously bucking the system, so to speak.

Reader reviews of *Twinkle — a memoir* were very good. I also heard from people about the effect the book had on them. Some could not finish reading it. Some had to break up the reading over months. Some — more than a few — asked me if everything I wrote really happened. It isn't that they didn't believe me. It was more that they had not encountered Evil so intimately, and they needed to confirm it was not them misunderstanding what was written.

For some, the girl in the book did not resemble the woman they had come to know.

But, look, let's not spoil your journey to how all that works out. So it is on that note that this introduction ends. You see, it is my hope that the emotional journey on the following pages will be tempered by first giving you a glimpse into the eventually bright future of that little girl. Also, while I danced around the role of God in the first book, threads binding me to Him and on which you will easily pick up, more specifically my Christian roots show in this introduction and afterword.

Angela K. Durden
January 2020

1987: My father Wesley is in the back row, far right. Aunt Pearl is front row, far
right, seated. These are the thirteen siblings on the Kell side who made it to
adulthood; one died young. As of this writing, all but Aunt Virginia (second row,
far left) have passed away. These are the people from whom I got my personality.
I got my twinkle from Daddy.

Twinkling for my stepfather in one of his
many photo sessions with me.

Twinkle— a memoir

The original 2015 book with a few additional photographs and captions and an occasional Author note bringing something to date. A new afterword follows.

Top: Author as firstborn. Bottom: Author as Big Sister.

Big Helper Becomes

You were born and were a happy child. Mother said so many times as she compared you to Little Sister, the red-faced screaming hellion who was never happy with anything hardly ever. So there you are, this happy child who loved her mother and wanted her to be proud of you and then one day she was.

You're such a big helper, she said the day you told her screaming sister's diaper was wet. From that moment your course in life is set, destiny defined, and the next eighteen years are spent being a big helper in ways your fifteen-monthold mind does not know exists. That begins in another year. In the meantime, you stand and stare at the red-faced alien. Somehow you know you're responsible for her.

You don't remember Daddy leaving. How did he pack his clothes? Did he hug you goodbye? Was there a big argument and he stormed out? Why did he leave you? Was he deployed and simply never came back? When will you see him again?

You don't know these things yet; but there will come a time when you will wish for Daddy with all your might, and a little girl's wishes are strong. There will come a time when you won't wish for him anymore. That's a sad day.

So you wake up on the sofa and feel the presence of what you later know to be evil. You look up into the eyes of a handsome devil, though a devil nonetheless. And, because you're a big helper and want to warn Mother, you scream and begin frantically to claw out of his arms. Smiling, he tries to hold you. Mother turns to the Devil and says she doesn't understand why her normally happy and smiling and helpful daughter is screaming and acting this way. She begs you, please be nice to my new friend, do this for me, please, it's important to me.

In places your little mind will not be able to access until years later, you know Mother is weak and needy and needs you to be The Big Helper and she needs it now. You stop screaming and say yes, Mama, turn to the Devil and smile with every twinkle you can muster.

The Devil falls in love and you know it.

And that is the day your life changes not for the better. The Devil makes a point of telling you how much he loves you. He wants to hold your hand. He takes you special places and Mother gets mad, but not at him. This is confusing.

So she takes you to her parents' house and drops you and Little Sister there. She does not visit. One day you'll look back at pictures from that year away from Weak Mother and Devil-Man and realize you were still a happy child and had little stress.

You remember walking to the store with Grandmother. You remember Grandfather. You remember choking on a butterscotch hard candy and being held upside down by one foot while you can't breathe and getting whacked on the back and watching the candy fall out of your throat. Grandmother threw it away because it hit the floor. You remember being sad you weren't going to be able to eat that candy and beginning a campaign to get another piece.

Grandmother refuses because she is convinced you will die. You stop asking Grandmother and begin a silent campaign toward Grandfather.

Grandfather refuses at first. He finally gives in but says you better not choke on it or else he'll get in trouble. You are very careful not to choke and that is a happy little secret you share. He will sneak you more hard candies through the years because you're The Big Helper who won't choke so that he won't get in trouble.

Back to the Devil

One year after Beloved Mother leaves you and Little Sister, she shows up out of the blue and takes you back to the Devil. He still loves you, though now he loves you more. You learn to control how you feel about him because Mother (mad because Devil likes you — a whole lot, too) still needs you to be nice. For her. Big Helper learns her job very, very well.

You look for more opportunities to save her because you know that is what you are doing. By now you see her beat, thrown around the house, not always successfully dodging plates and ketchup bottles and coffee cups.

You help her clean up broken dishes. You wash ketchup off the walls. And you ask yourself how you can stop Devil from hurting Beloved But Weak Mother. It takes time to figure it out. Sadness and madness and violence is against your nature yet you must study it, must understand it. You must!

And with each cup hurled, with each slap to her face, with each thud of her body hitting the floor, you pour equal measures of thought and observation and analytical power into the problem.

Then one day Devil calls you into the bedroom, the one he sleeps in with Beloved Mother. You're in the kitchen and don't want to go into the bedroom with Devil. You don't like to do that. But Mother, still mad at you, says angrily he is calling and you must go.

You walk toward the bedroom knowing what it is you must do.

You must pretend to like it. You must be convincing. This lying is against your nature, but you do it because you are The Big Helper and Mother needs you to smile, so you smile. And you twinkle with all your might when with the Devil.

You must make Devil happy so he won't beat Beloved But Weak Mother. And Devil is happy and says this is how married people do it. And you bounce up and down and make happy noises and show teeth in a smile and twinkle eyes as fast as they can twinkle and Devil is happy.

Midnight on a Texas Back Road

One night, Devil's seventh wife and you and Little Sister and Big Baby Brother are in a car going very, very fast down a dark Texas back road. Beloved Mother screams for Devil to slow down and he slaps her hard, punching, shoving, jerking her head around using her hair as a handle. You kids watching from the back seat, as usual.

Devil tells her over and over to shut the fuck up but she just won't, and he gets madder and madder until, finally, he screeches to a stop in the highway, leans across her and opens the door. She claws to stay in, but he kicks her until she's shoved to the ground on her butt. He screams get your little bastards out and you three climb over the seat as best you can and get shoved out, too, because you aren't fast enough for him.

He closes the door and takes off. You hear him screaming above the roar of the engine. Another car comes upon the scene; it stops. Two men say to Beloved Mother for her to quick, quick, get in the car with the kids and we'll take you all to safety. Their words have barely registered with her, though you see the wisdom in their suggestion and look to Beloved Mother for a rational decision, when you hear an engine roaring and turn to look. It's Devil! He's backing down the highway to Beloved Mother and her little bastards. The men beg her to get in the car with the kids. We'll save you, they plead.

She stares back and forth from them to her returning torturer. The taillights come closer and you think they will run you over. You are terrified more than you've ever been terrified before. You want to jump in the other car and go, go, go. Beloved Mother does nothing and you wait to be smashed flat because you must stay with her.

Devil stops, throws the door open, and says nobody's going to give his woman and kids a ride, so get the fuck in the car. The men watch helplessly as you climb back in the car in reverse order from which you were shoved; they can do nothing. Devil guns the engine and takes off into the night screaming hitchhiking whore looking for men to fuck can't wait to get it can you, and punches and slaps Beloved Mother and you kids sit in the back seat and watch as his fist full of her hair whips her head against the dash.

As usual.

Twinkling at the Christmas Party

Christmas party. Devil's house. You're…five or six? Five. You're under the chairs in the living room, giggling with Little Sister, crawling from chair to chair. A glass is set on the floor, you race her to get to it and drink what is in it. Little Sister is smaller and faster, or you let her win, you don't remember, but she gets most of the drinks, this you do remember. She gets stone drunk. Only you don't know why she is acting like that. You've never seen her this giggly, this happy, this shiny, this…dancy?

Music penetrates Little Sister's brain, and she crawls out from under the chairs, and dances. She is wild, pulling up her dress and showing her panties and singing and twirling and bumping into people and things. She is twinkling badly; her twinkling will get her in trouble. She will be in trouble soon because Devil doesn't like Little Sister and this is Devil's party. His friends are laughing at the little, drunk, twirling girl so violence is not immediate. The laughter doesn't last long though because they want to laugh and be happy and dance in their own way, and her entertainment is not what they want.

Devil is getting tired of it, looks at Beloved Mother and sighs, and she looks to you. You don't miss your cue. Crawling out from under the chairs, you begin to dance wildly. You sing. You twirl. You show your panties. You twinkle better than Little Sister and soon all eyes are on you, as you knew they would be, and as you enjoy because you're in control of this not-so-controlled situation. You take Little Sister's hand and bow together — to enthusiastic applause — then hustle her out of the room. Beloved Mother relaxes.

The Atheist Devil's Christmas

Christmas Day comes. On this particular one there are lots of presents. They are opened. There is general subdued excitement over toys. Soon you hear Beloved Mother begging: Honey, please don't make her do that, she'll get cut. You are called over anyway. It is time to take down the Christmas tree for Devil, the Atheist. You are told to put the ornaments on the floor and smash them with your bare feet. Little Sister thinks this is grand fun. She does not understand the danger and you both smash balls beneath your feet, you praying the whole time you don't get cut because by now you know something else.

You don't like pain. And you pray. Beloved Mother must have said something about talking to God and even though you don't know anything about Him, you know you can say things in your mind and He hears them. This is a comfort and you pray for the first time as you smash those glass balls.

Please, God, don't let me get cut.

Stomp, smash, twinkle, laugh to please Devil, the Atheist.

Please, God, don't let me get cut.

Stomp, smash, twinkle, laugh to please Devil.

Please, please, God, please, I don't want to get cut. Please, God? Please?

Stomp, smash, twinkle, twinkle, twinkle, laugh to please Devil as you silently implore God, his enemy, your friend you hope, for help.

For the first time in your life you feel guilty because you not once mention Little Sister's feet. This prayer is all about you. This is a bad, very bad thing to do, but you don't, not once, think of her because you're so scared of the blood you might see and you don't want to see the blood, you don't want to see the blood because it terrifies you.

Guilt tears at you. You know Christmas will come again and you will have to smash glass again. What can you do to think of Little Sister during this time and not be so worried about yourself? It takes a few months and it is Beloved Mother who supplies the answer. She is taking a splinter out of your finger with a sewing needle. You see her pick at it until the splinter comes out and you squeeze your finger to stop the pain and, ah — blood!

You can get used to blood by making yourself bleed. You watch where the needle is put up and when no one is looking, go get it. But where to make blood show without anyone noticing? Belly button. You go into a room by yourself and close the door. Sitting on the bed, you begin to dig into your belly button. Lint comes out and the belly button is clean. You are horrified your belly button has that much dirt in it and almost forget why you're there.

Oh, yeah. Blood. Where is the blood? You dig deeper and the blood comes out. You watch it. You feel the pain, and study it. You make it hurt worse

and want to throw up. Suddenly you're across the room, floating in the corner of the ceiling, watching someone else do this thing to your belly button. You see this other little girl dig harder and deeper. Now you feel again and you aren't near the ceiling. Beloved Mother comes in the room and screams quietly. She takes away the needle. You aren't finished yet! You get mad at Beloved Mother. She puts a Band-Aid on the spot and begs you not to tell Honey — Devil — because she will get in trouble if you're hurt.

You spend a lot of time over the next few years cleaning out your belly button — you can't stand how filthy it gets — and practicing making blood and enduring the pain. You never get caught again.

Horse Leaves You

Badge Man is in the yard behind the house. He pulls out his gun. You run into a bedroom, Little Sister and Baby Brothers behind you. Wedging yourself into a corner, they pile into the safety of your arms. They cling and cry and you try to comfort them.

Horse's jaw is locked. Why can't they use a key and unlock it instead of killing Horse? No one can answer and they say Horse must die. So Badge Man shoots Horse. At the shot, the huddle in the bedroom corner jumps as one and the babies scream.

Horse falls. You don't see it, but you hear its body hit the ground; you know that sound. The huddle and you cry and wail because Horse is killed. A truck takes Horse away. You watch the big truck pull away with Horse piled in the back. Horse doesn't hear the screams as you run behind the truck.

Horse! Horse! Come back, Horse! Don't leave me, Horse.

Devil is sad Horse is dead, but he's more sad because you're sad. He puts his arm around you and promises to get another horse to make you happy again. He likes for you to smile; smile for Honey. He needs you to twinkle. He gets another horse; you like it okay. Devil expects to be rewarded for his effort at making you happy and, hiding the pain, you twinkle and smile and jump up and down with happy claps. Devil struts away, a man happy to have proof of his manhood. See, he made a woman happy. He fixed her problem and she twinkled. Isn't he simply a marvelous male?

You still miss Horse and never forget him — at least not for a very long time — and you never forgive Devil for having him killed.

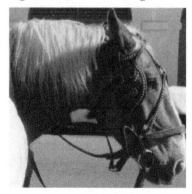

Takes a Lickin' and Keeps on Tickin'

Grandfather's visits were fun. You use the word fun now because you know fun, but then you didn't. Still, you liked it when he visited. One day he shows up and calls you and Little Sister to him. He has a present for both of you.

You're worried it's going to be something you'll have to share because if you have to share it, then Little Sister will claim it as hers and you will never get to play with it. If there is one each, then maybe she'll leave your toy alone. Only today Grandfather doesn't have a toy.

He hands each of you a box like you've never seen before. Open it, he says. Go on, open it. He smiles. You both ask what it is. He waggles his fingers at the boxes. Open. Go on, open.

There's a watch, shiny silver with one word written on it. You can't read yet, but you know it's a word and before even saying thank you, ask what this word is. Grandfather is pleased.

Timex, he says. He laughs and says it takes a lickin' and keeps on tickin'.

Grandfather explains you're holding watches. He helps you put them on and admire them. He explains how they work, what they're for. Furthermore, he warns you not to lose them because they cost a lot of money. You both nod gravely and set about learning to tell time.

The next time Grandfather visits he asks where your watch is. You look at your wrist, then at him, and say you don't know. He turns to Little Sister and checks her wrist. Her watch is still there. Do you not know where your watch is?

You can't tell him. You just know one day it was there and then one day it wasn't. Did you lose it? You don't know. Is it in your bedroom? You don't know. Does Mother have it? By now you're quite worried about this thing. Grandfather says he'll buy another, but you must promise, promise, promise not to lose it.

You have to think about that.

He does not understand why you can't answer right away, but you don't want to promise something you cannot do. You finally answer and he shakes his head as he says aaaahhh...okay. He drives to the store and buys another Timex.

You will make sure you don't lose this one and solemnly put it on your wrist. After all, these are very expensive and you shouldn't waste Grandfather's money.

On his next visit, you inform him that watch disappeared, too. He doesn't understand why and you don't either. One day it's there and one day it isn't. Nothing else to say.

Angie....aaaahhh — and off he goes to buy you another. After several Timex watches go missing in action, there comes a time when he tells you he isn't buying you any more until you learn to be responsible like Little Sister, whose watch is still on her wrist.

Little Sister holds out her wrist and gives you the ha-ha look even while you know she wants to lose hers because she wants more gifts, but she never can seem to lose that damn watch.

Finally, in your forties, you stop wearing a watch because it was getting expensive to keep one on your wrist; they kept flying off. Strangers chase you down in the mall and give you the watch you didn't know had come off. Or you find it in the yard a few weeks later. Often you never find them at all.

One day, while Grandfather was still buying Timex watches, you asked him why it was that people licked watches.

Chuckling as he shakes his head, he tries to explain, can't, and ends with Angie...aaaahh — a phrase you will hear from many men throughout your life.

Top: Grandfather as a Marine.
Bottom: Author (at back) with Little Sister and Big Baby Brother.

The Analyst

Around this time Mother gets religion though Devil is a French Canadian Catholic Atheist haunted by what he thinks is the spirit of his dead sister, the one he murdered — accidentally, so he says — when she's fourteen and he's eleven.

Devil doesn't seem to understand: Without God he doesn't exist.

On the other hand, you believe in a higher power because you want to believe. You just don't know *what* to believe. Mother's foray into religion this time doesn't last but a year before she gives up on it. But you don't; this inner spiritual core needs feeding and you wonder where a person goes to find out about this God that's so strong Devil's sister's spirit never comes back again.

He must be strong. You need Him to be strong. God remains elusive for some years, though you continue to study Devil. Then you add another subject to your study: Mother. What is it she does that sets Devil off so? Why does she enjoy the beatings?

Oh, yes. She enjoys them, enjoys them very much. Somehow the pain is like a drug to her. You know this because she tells you all the stories and you see the twinkle even though she is crying.

You don't play like other children do. Intent on the game, you run fast. Hit balls hard. Kick balls farther. Run and catch whatever is thrown your way. Your instincts for being in the right place at the right time on the field make you one of the most valuable players and you're always picked at the beginning when teams are divided up. In the game, you never laugh, never smile.

Intense.

You stare at the field of play, anticipating where the next ball will go and you're usually right. Analytical thought will come in handy at school. However, that happens some years later.

For now, there you are, out in the yard, throwing stones, bouncing a ball, riding a bike, and Mother calls you in or comes home from her most current job at a honky-tonk and you can tell she is ready for a chat.

You steel your six-year-old mind for whatever it is she will tell you today.

Will it be another gang rape in the back of a car while Devil holds a knife to her throat and lets each man have her in turn? Will it be about yet another man she had sex with because he was really nice? She asks for your advice on more than one occasion and you give it. You are not surprised she takes it because by now you realize something else about Mother.

She isn't very smart. Oh, she can do things, lots of things. She can read and understand. She learns new jobs quickly and is always one of the best employees. But for all her brains, she isn't very smart about life and she has a memory problem, too. She's always surprised when a man is bad or uses then discards her. Her sadness would make you worried for her more except for one thing: She is never sad about what you are going through. Or your sister or brothers for that matter, though she does say it is your job to worry about them and to be sad for them.

Don't have enough food, Mama. Nothing can be done, she says, he takes all my money. Got hurt, Mama. Can't go to the doctor, she says, he won't let us go. Shoes too small, Mama. Let's hope Grandmother brings some soon.

The excuses are different, the results the same. Ah. The key to all this is Devil and you study him more closely. How can you get food and clothes for Baby Brothers and Little Sister? Their eyes turn to you and they wait. You find a way without Devil knowing.

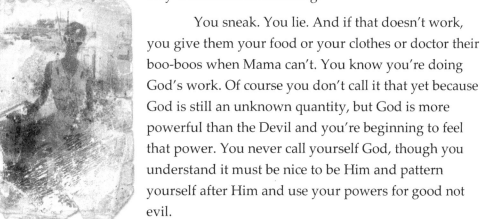

You sneak. You lie. And if that doesn't work, you give them your food or your clothes or doctor their boo-boos when Mama can't. You know you're doing God's work. Of course you don't call it that yet because God is still an unknown quantity, but God is more powerful than the Devil and you're beginning to feel that power. You never call yourself God, though you understand it must be nice to be Him and pattern yourself after Him and use your powers for good not evil.

And still Devil loves you while Beloved Mother hates you for that love.

Left Behind

When you were six and still living in Texas, Devil said you needed to learn a lesson. Devil always wanted to teach you something. So, anyway, he said you will never, ever see Little Sister, Beloved Mother, Baby Brothers, or him ever again. They are leaving. Beloved Mother frowned and you thought she was frowning at you, yet you didn't care.

Everybody got in the car and Devil stood by it, suitably dramatic of course, and made everyone wave to you from the car as he said they were leaving, never to return. He got in and off they went, and the car got smaller and smaller, then disappeared.

At first there was worry. How would Beloved Mother and everybody else be able to live without your twinkling for Devil? Then you smiled.

You smiled and laughed and skipped through the house and found the melty mints and for each one you gave the Froot Loops bird in his cage, you ate one until the whole bag was gone. Then you listened to him clunk his beaks together and make that noise you like as he begged for more.

You went into the refrigerator and found more food — and ate it.

You skipped and played and listened to the quiet, happier than ever in the first peace you knew was yours forever and ever. Alone, at last, for the first time. No one to torture you. No one to ask for anything. No one to scream at you or hit you. No one to save. No one to twinkle for.

Peace. And the day wore on and darkness came. You hear a noise. It sounds like...no. It can't be.

A car pulls up. You peek through a curtain and your world, your peaceful, solitary world, crashes. You sit in a chair, wait, and watch, eyes steady on the front door. You know what's going to happen and it does.

Devil slings the door open, dramatically of course, wags a finger and says he hopes you learned your lesson. Oh, you learned it all right. You never forget it.

Later that evening Devil wants to know why all the melty mints are gone. He accuses you of being selfish and not wanting to share. You calmly explain that, per his earlier proclamation, you were never going to see them ever again, and since they were never coming back and you got hungry…

You twinkle your logic; Devil blinks in wonder — and falls in love more.

Little Sister is mad because she didn't get left behind so she could eat melty mints, too, and dogs your every step, fussing that you should have saved her some. Froot Loops bird got sick and that worried Devil; you never told Devil you fed him half the mints.

You knew when to keep your mouth shut.

Devil with arm around Author. Author with arm around Little
Sister. In front of Author: Little Baby Brother.
In front of Devil: Big Baby Brother.

Devil-Men

Sitting outside one summer, letting all your energy go into thinking about a problem, you notice something. What is that on your right foot? You're surprised to see a very long scar running from the tip of the little toe halfway up the side. You study it as if it is not your foot.

Forty years later you get around to asking Beloved Mother about how the scar got there. She tells a tale about a Coke bottle she kicked when she got mad at Devil and the Coke bottle somehow landed on your foot and mysteriously shattered and ripped it open. You ask if this is the time you were in the hospital when you were four. She says yes and is surprised you remember the hospital stay. As if you could ever forget it.

Held down by three women, you hear a doctor screaming over and over keep her still as he hurts your foot, squeezing it hard. All you can do is scream and fight and claw and kick and try to bite. You must escape this pain and these people. Why are you here? Why are they doing this? You have no idea. This is not what you most remember about the hospital stay, though.

You never see Beloved Mother during the whole event and later that night wake up in a hospital bed and there is Little Sister, sound asleep beside you.
Beloved Mother must have needed an evening out with Honey, so she left Little Sister for you to babysit, as usual. You wake up because you feel something sharp. Then your legs are spread apart. Oh, no. Devil is here. You feel something between your legs. You try to move but your body will not. You open your eyes but it isn't Devil standing over the bed.

It's a man. In a white coat. You don't know him. He is breathing hard and you feel his finger inside you over and over and harder and harder and he is breathing just like Devil does. You feel a pain, but it's like feeling a pain through a blanket. You concentrate on that and wonder about it. Little Sister moans in her sleep and rolls over with her back to you, settles in close, like she's snuggling, and you're happy she doesn't see this. You wait for the man to touch her, but he never does. He is in love with you just like Devil. It is on this night you learn there are other devil-men, and they can be anywhere, and you never forget.

In your head, you scream so loud the whole world can hear. In your head, you fight so hard the new devil-man dies. He does. You see him dead on the floor — in your head. You promise yourself *this* will never happen again — *this* meaning being unable to respond to the emergency situation and control it. So you shut up in your mind and you stop fighting in your mind and you coldly watch the new devil-man and study him.

Yes, you watch as he finishes with you, pulls your little gown down, covers you with a blanket, pats your head, rubs the front of his pants some more, turns and walks out.

You turn eyes toward Little Sister. Did she hear anything? Did she see anything? Satisfied she was asleep during the entire event, you feel

better because by now you know something about her. She's weak like Beloved Mother. They both need you to take pain for them. Seemingly you have a high tolerance for pain of some kinds, and you do your job well even though pain scares you worse than anything.

Anyway, you forgot how you got the scar because the other pain was worse: The pain of not being in control. Your mission, your aim, your goal from this point, besides protecting Beloved Mother and Little Sister and Baby Brothers, is to always be in control of the weak people surrounding you so you can minimize their opportunities to bring pain. You begin the further study of how to do that. Because by now you understand something else.

Soaring, Grace, and Power

Yes, by now you understand Beloved Mother somehow manages to bring extra trouble on herself because she says the wrong thing. Always. How is it she doesn't remember from one time to the next what makes Devil mad? It becomes too much for your brain to understand. One morning when you're five or six, you wake with a feeling of happiness and lightness and you're smiling the smile of the innocent and strong.

Beloved Mother is hanging clothes on the line outside. You rush out the door screaming Mama! Mama! You tell her you can breathe underwater. She says that is impossible. But you've done it, you say. She smiles sadly. You will prove it, you say confidently, emphatically, with an assuredness of fact known and proved.

It must be summer, and before she can say anything, you run to the small plastic pool full of hot dirty water, jump in, submerse yourself, and breathe deeply.

You come up in a second, choking and gagging. Mother says she told you so, but her voice is vague because you're wondering why it was last night you could do this and now you cannot. You are not yet aware of the unreal nature of dreams because you know they are real. They are, or how else could you know what it is like to fly high above the earth riding the waves of the wind, light and free and graceful, while watching the family below? Or feel the grace of the dolphin as it cuts through the water and jumps high and splashes into the waves? How else could you know the power the stallion feels — not the mare, never the damn mare — as it runs confident, strong, beautiful across the prairie?

So, yes, you can too breathe underwater and swim under it light and free and graceful. Something merely went wrong with this try. You will figure it out and when you do, you'll show Beloved Mother and she will be proud of you again, maybe.

When you're married and have children of your own, you find a picture of yourself and Little Sister standing side by side in front of the barn. You have on shorts with holsters holding little pop-cap pistols, skinny legs stuffed into boots. This picture is serious business. You're not sure why now, but it was, so you didn't smile when it was taken.

You had not thought of those days in a long time. Seeing your serious little face with Little Sister beside you opens doors to rooms in your mind and you won't be able to shut those doors again for years.

Cocktails and Dancing

First First-Grade Teacher calls your name. You look up from curling strips of paper for Santa's beard. She says to get your things. You look past her and see Beloved Mother. Teacher is not happy at your leaving. She hugs you and says she will miss you. You silently walk past her holding half-bearded Santa, and follow silent Beloved Mother. You never go back to that school.

The family is moving. Devil, or Honey as you've now been instructed to call him, is moving to take yet another job. Such moves always coincide with staying one step ahead of the law. When Honey got out of prison after a fourteen year stretch, he jumped parole by leaving Oklahoma and went to Texas where he spotted Beloved Mother.

He was always in trouble for doing something dangerous or dumb. So you move. Beloved Mother begins another job at a honky-tonk and Honey becomes the bartender. He likes to go in on his days off and take you, you know, like a date. One night you sit like a regal queen with him at a table, sipping a delicious cocktail as a lady should who is waiting for the show to begin: Pinky outstretched, spine ramrod straight. Lights dim, music starts, every man looks at the stage. Honey says to watch because there is a surprise for you.

A naked woman walks out wearing three things: Two high-heeled shoes and your pet boa constrictor, Snake. She dances badly, and she has these ugly things hanging off the front of her chest flopping around. She is afraid of Snake, though she asked to borrow him to keep men's hands away during her act. You know her and don't like her. She spends a lot of time at your house. She and Beloved Mother are always spitting at each other like a couple of cats because Beloved Mother has to wait on her hand and foot while Naked Woman snuggles up with Honey.

You watch her act closely and study the men. Conclusions? They are all devil-men and you can control them. You must control them, and her, because you must save Snake who loves you and Snake is not happy right now. You know this because when Snake is with you, Snake likes to snuggle. He wraps himself around your waist, climbs your back, and puts his head behind your ear and stays there for hours and hours, content. You love Snake and Snake loves you and you know he is unhappy with Naked Woman. You must save Snake from her and the devil-men who are slapping at him. He can't escape, though he tries and she has a hard time holding him.

You sip the cocktail, thinking of what to do and the plan soon becomes clear. You get up in the chair and climb to the top of the table. You stamp feet apart and holler loud to be heard over the music: I can dance better than that!

Naked Woman stops dancing. All the devil-men look at you. You show them how much better you can dance. They clap and whistle. Naked Woman is furious and stomps off the stage, no one paying attention to her flopping self. She never comes back to the house and Snake is happy. Honey loves you. Oh, how he loves you. He looks around at his friends, accepting the applause as his own. Honey likes the way you dance. You will do it again other times for him and his friends.

In you, Honey thinks he has found his soul mate. He teaches you how to lie, though he doesn't know you're already good at it. He teaches you how to steal, though he doesn't know you already know that, too. You let him teach these lessons and twinkle at him and say how smart he is and every little girl should be so lucky to have such a Honey and he beams and struts.

God Understands About Lying

By now you've learned something about how to control devil-men, several of whom you've met. You have it all figured out by the time you're seven. Stroke his ego, and he will be under your control. Sincerity is key. He must believe you truly feel he is the most handsome, most smart, most strong, most manly, most virile man in the whole wide world. You, who hates lying, learn how to lie with eyes wide, clear, unblinking.

This you know for a certainty: God understands that to lie to devil-men is not wrong. With a smile and a clear conscience, you stroke and twinkle, but only to save Beloved Mother or Little Sister or Baby Brothers. Somehow it seems almost wrong to twinkle on behalf of yourself, but you cheat occasionally, feeling guilty the whole time.

You refine this method by trial and error, though, and sometimes don't do such a good job and Devil gets mad. You learn quickly so as to never repeat a mistake. Beloved Mother is doing a fine job of showing you what doesn't work, so you never do any of that, doing the opposite, watching, building your first relational database of scenarios, times of day or year, and responses until there is a whole catalog to guide the smooth, workable methodology of everyday survival.

When you're in fourth grade, you try your method on another man, the daddy of a girl you want to come visit your house. His head snaps around when you call him Daddy in the voice you know works with devil-men. He won't let his daughter come visit. You are surprised he does not do your bidding and stare at him, studying. He stares back, but not with the devil-man stare of flirting and sizing up opportunity.

No, this man is worried, and categorically refuses to allow his daughter to go; why you do not know. The confusing response is cataloged and returned to for study again and again.

Years later you realize this was a good man, protecting his daughter, and you wish for a daddy like that; by then it's too late for real daddies.

For now you know all men are devil-men except Grandfather, who still happily sneaks you butterscotches even though Grandmother is no longer around to fuss at him. You don't learn until you're in your twenties they got divorced. You thought Grandmother was driving around the country visiting friends and taking long, long vacations, popping in occasionally with clothes and presents.

Oh, goody. Grandfather is coming to visit. Beloved Mother said he is going to pick you up from school today. Treat! Because every day you must walk through a field, staying clear of the bulls. The school is directly behind the field. You wait in the afternoon and Grandfather isn't there when you think he should be, so you walk along the dusty Texas road because that is where he'll be driving. You will meet him.

You walk a long way down the wrong road though you don't know it's the wrong road, and walk and walk and it's getting later and later and then you hear a truck come up from behind and hear Grandfather say to get in. Never scared, you knew you would meet him on the road. He asks what you're doing walking on the road. You say he was late and you went to get him.

He smiles sadly as he begins to say something, changes his mind — Angie….aaaaahhhh — and says not to tell Mother. Another happy secret to think about a lot.

Twinkling for Food

You awaken one morning very early to an urgent voice. Quick, someone says, get in the car. You rub the sleepy out of your eyes and stumble to the car, stretch out in the back seat, and fall asleep. Two-hundred miles later you wake up because Little Sister is whispering in your ear.

Do you want a cookie? You want a cookie? You can't have a cookie. Honey says these cookies are all his so hands off. Ha, ha, hahahahaha.

You reach down in the floorboard and pick up the Chips Ahoy bag, open it and, one by one, slowly eat every cookie even though you get sick. With each quiet reach into the bag Little Sister whispers you're gonna get in trouble, yet her eyes say she can't wait for you to get beat like she sometimes does when you aren't around to run interference.

You know you won't get in trouble, though. Before too long, Honey asks for the bag of cookies; he's hungry and needs a snack. Running from the law makes a man hungry. Little Sister hands him the empty bag with a flourish of righteousness. Her glance your way says now Big Sister will get hers. Honey screams and curses and, keeping his left hand on the wheel, flings his right fist toward Little Sister over the back of the seat.

She dodges his blows and from the farthest corner of the back seat screams she isn't the one who ate them and points at you, now sitting and staring at him in the rearview mirror. You twinkle and he melts. Oh, he says, okay, and he turns and drives, his mad all gone away.

Little Sister, in the back seat, and Beloved Mother, in the front, fling stares at you. You're not sure what the expressions on their faces are, but you know it ain't good for you. You become very familiar with those looks and they bode ill each time they are flung.

Nonprofit Arson

You get to a place called Florida and settle in yet another new house. Babysitter comes along on the trip. You don't like Babysitter; he is a devil-man who is in love with you, too. Babysitter hates Little Sister and Baby Brothers. He washes out Big Baby Brother's mouth with soap — you scream while he does it — and he says the boy must be taught a lesson about using bad language. Big Baby Brother said damn and for that his mouth was soaped with hot water. You watch him gag and fight against Babysitter and you can't stop Babysitter. You feel helpless and wonder why Babysitter is a devil-man who won't do what you want right now. You study the situation because you will never let Babysitter do that again to Big Baby Brother. It was wrong.

It is now you begin to formulate an opinion about justice. Though you don't know that word yet, you know Babysitter completely done wrong by Big Baby Brother and begin to hate him more. So you pour on the twinkling and keep his attention away from Little Sister, who he hits, and Baby Brothers, who he likes to torture. Your ramped-up campaign works.

But, how to get rid of him? You don't know. And here he is on the trip.

Years later you ask Beloved Mother about that Florida time. She, who usually tells you everything, never mentioned the story. Well, it seems the law never came looking for them, so she tells you — chuckling as if it was such a lark while, having again found religion, bringing in a note of righteous indignation — that she had been forced by Honey to help burn down a honky-tonk.

That Florida time was hiding-from-the-law time. Beloved Mother and Honey did such a bad job that everyone knew who did it and who hired them and thus they were forced to leave Texas overnight. Everything is sold, including Snake. Again something that loved you is ripped away and you have no say. Beloved Mother gets a job at a respectable restaurant in Florida — she could wear all her clothes when she went to work — and makes good tip money. You know because each night she empties out pockets and purses onto a table and Honey counts it and pockets it and leaves.

One day she came home, furious. The man who hired them found her at the restaurant and said she and Honey would not get paid for the arson because the place was only damaged and the insurance company said it will be repaired.

Three months into hiding out, she calls her daddy, Grandfather, who sends money for the family to move back to Georgia. Grandfather said he would not send any money for Babysitter and Babysitter must not come. Then Babysitter is gone and you never have to worry about him again, though you never forget there are some devil-men who need a higher level of attention to be controlled. Beloved Mother laughs when she tells the story, though you don't see the humor.

So, now you're back in the state where you were born. Grandfather buys a trailer, one bedroom, one bath, and builds bunk beds in the living room and puts curtains around them, and parks it in a nice trailer park, and there are a lot of kids around, and a creek, and a lake, and a pool, a clean pool that you do not try to breathe underwater in, and lots of bumps on the hill coming down to the trailer. You love to ride the neighbor boy's bike over the bumps you learn are called speed breakers, though you don't know why because they help you go faster. You start a new school, finish first grade, then hear about this great thing: Vacation Bible School. Finally, a chance to learn about God.

Vacation Bible School

Vacation Bible School. It's free. They pick you up in a bus. They take you to a church where you can learn about God. Beloved Mother signs up you and Little Sister.

The first day you spend coloring pictures. You color patiently and say nothing. The second day you spend coloring pictures. Your patience is running out and you ask when you will learn about God. The lady stares as if you are speaking in tongues. The third day you are not a happy Vacation Bible School camper and refuse to color. They nag: Color! Color! Jesus wants you to color!

Your reply is swift: I came here to learn about God and now I want to learn about God, goddammit.

The teachers are shocked and the pastor is called. They huddle at the door of the room in which you insist to be taught about God; they confab with quiet desperation, and fear. Nobody knows what to do with you. You spend the rest of the day sitting, stubbornly refusing to color or drink or eat or play. The bus comes and you go home and refuse to go back. Beloved Mother asks why. You thoroughly and passionately explain you went there to learn about God and they wouldn't tell you anything and you will not go back if they can't do their job because it is a waste of time.

She stares and says nothing.

She doesn't know what to do with you either.

Honey Dies. Devil Lives.

Second grade starts. Little Sister enters first grade and you help her find her room. You think she is supposed to be in Second First-Grade Teacher's room; you're wrong and there is a bit of confusion as she takes a seat in a fifth-grade class. You eventually find the correct room and drop her off, again.

Little Sister's teacher hates her and spanks her and hits her hands with a flat ruler and Beloved Mother comes to the school and has an argument with the teacher. Little Sister is never touched again though you're happy she got beat because you know she needs it, often begs for it, and truthfully you would like for her to get beat more. You always wanted what's best for her.

Anyway, you come home from school one day and Honey says he is dying. He calls you to his side and you see blood dripping out of his mouth and down his shirt. Beloved Mother is in the kitchen and she is mad, this time at Honey; this is a first. This is serious. You turn back to him.

You stand next to Honey and weep and wail as he tells the tale of his dying. He will go into the woods, yes, yes, he will. And he'll lie down like the Indians and die as one with nature, yes, yes, indeed he will. You are so sad Honey is dying because you love Honey. He takes you places. He teaches you things. He smiles when he sees you. You know the other things he does, but when Honey comes out, you try to forget Devil.

Honey staggers to the door. He gives an emotional goodbye. You weep — sincerely and deeply. Loss is hard for you. Then, oh then you think about what he needs and become resolute. Determined to honor his death, you give him a look a fallen Indian warrior would be proud of. He leaves in the only car the family has.

Beloved Mother is furious. Little Sister is happy and Baby Brothers don't understand. You are sad, sadder than at any time in your little life. You've lost another thing that loves you. Even if that love is not always good, when it is good, you're very happy and feel cherished. Horse is gone. Snake is gone. Now Honey is leaving.

You go to school; teachers notice something wrong and they ask. You tell them the tale of Honey's dying. Oh, oh, oh, about Honey bleeding from his mouth, blood dripping down his shirt, and going to die in the woods like his ancestors, the Indians. Teachers stare at you, then look at each other. One says your daddy is not dead. *He is not my daddy,* you say, he is my stepfather, with a mighty strong emphasis on *step*. You give them the long story about your real daddy coming to get you one day. Teachers simply nod, and you walk away to continue grieving.

Two more days pass and the grieving is over. You've made plans for the rest of what life you might have; these plans do not include Devil nor Honey. You feel a lightness about your heart and mind and you smile and play and comfort Beloved Mother; she won't get beat no more, so smile, be happy. She smiles sadly and says nothing. Little Sister and Baby Brothers are free and run and play like they always do but now they shout and laugh and wrassle happily. You survey the happy home and know the rest of your life will be good with Devil gone.

The next day you come home from school and notice the car is there. You open the door to step into your now happy and relaxed home. The same car Honey drove away in brought Devil back. Devil smiles and says surprise, he didn't die and he laughs about how he fooled everybody and isn't this just the best joke ever?

In a split second you size up the situation. Beloved Mother is in the kitchen. Little Sister stands beside you with a blank stare. Baby Brothers, not yet in school and already familiar with his resurrection, run and play with no laughter. Devil is expecting a reaction from you. He waits for it. He craves it. He needs it, and he needs it now. He's been waiting for it all these days.

You, who thought you wouldn't have to use your twinkle again, fake the biggest, sincerest twinkle of your life to date. Your heart is dead; your analytical mind takes over. Honey is happy with the quality and amount and content of the twinkle. He gives Beloved Mother a look, triumphant of his restored manhood, and Beloved Mother gets mad — at you.

Devil would celebrate his happiness with you later

.

The First Thanksgiving

When you live at the trailer park, the owners of the park are very rich. You know this because they lived in something called a double-wide and inside was a fountain. A real fountain with running water and goldfish swimming in the little pool at the bottom. Inside their trailer. And the rich lady wore lots of rings on her fat fingers and she crocheted jewelry out of ropes of pearly looking things and sold it and made a lot of money.

For some reason, they liked Honey and Beloved Mother and all the kids and they cooked a feast for Thanksgiving. Never in your little life had you seen so much food in one place. You did not know what most of it was, but it was food, and your nose was filled with the unknown scents of deliciousness, and you couldn't wait to eat.

The rich, fat-fingered lady kept saying to eat, eat! You just couldn't after a while because you were full. Of course, before you were allowed to eat, the rich man said a prayer you thought would never end. He told God things you were sure God knew about Himself and then the rich man said he was proud for the bounty God set before them and you wondered which of the things on the table was bounty because you recognized the turkey and thought you recognized the green beans, though they looked fancy cooked, but the rest of the food was a mystery. So why would he only thank God for the bounty and not for the turkey and green beans, too?

Amens said, you dig in, fork flying, until your eyeballs are floating on a sea of warm gravy filling your little tummy and you are...what are you? Happy? Hmmm...you will have to think on this new sensation, but it is duly cataloged.

Dirty Dancing

Honey brings home a present for you, a present you like. New clothes are rare and here you are, presented with these new pajamas, soft, pretty, and very thin. You feel like a movie star and tell Honey how much you like them. You genuinely like your new pajamas and your excitement at getting such a nice present, only for you, is evident. It makes you feel warm, even loved. Honey tells you to wear them to bed and you do. Little Sister is mad because she didn't get any new pajamas and the bed you share gets smaller as she gets madder. You both fall asleep.

Some hours later, you aren't sure how many, you feel a nudge on your shoulder. Honey whispers for you to get up. He has another surprise. He helps you out of the top bunk bed and you slide into the small living room, the same living room he was dying in the other week. There are several men sitting in chairs in a circle. Some you know because you play with their children up the street; some are strangers.

They look as you are presented with a flourish and the introductions begin. Look at her pajamas, Devil tells the men. Nice, huh? The men look you over from head to toe and nod in silent, intense agreement. You stand straight and tall and look the men in the eye one by one.

A little lamp is put on the floor and the shade is taken off. You are placed in front of the lamp. Now the pajamas, thin and light and so very much loved for their prettiness, become dirty to you.

You don't use the word dirty, you just know you don't like them anymore and you want them off and want to take a bath. You will assign the word dirty at a later date.

Devil tells you to dance. There is no music being played, so you listen to the music in your head. The men stare, solemn and bright-eyed and breathless, as you dance and dance and —

As you wait in the line for the school bus the next morning, you chat with the boy of a daddy who was there the previous night. You tell him you saw his daddy. The boy wants to know why his daddy was at your house. You say you danced for him.

That evening you learn a further lesson about keeping your mouth shut. Not a hard lesson to learn because Honey politely explains the man got in trouble with his wife because she doesn't like dancing not one bit. You're shocked and so sorry you talked. Gently, nobly, he forgives you, but you keep even quieter from then on. Shhhh…*wink*…our little secret, okay?

Little Con

Devil, or Honey — you're confused about this point — bestows upon you a title: Little Con. The lessons in lying and stealing continue and he finds you a quick study and very adept at applying those lessons. He couldn't have been prouder if you were his own flesh and blood. Beloved Mother sighs and leaves the room. On the other hand, you're enthralled. Devil teaches the lesson, but it's Honey who's proud. You love the positive attention. It's something you don't get a lot of and you sure do need a lot of attention.

Now, where to practice what you are learning? Ah. School. Perfect.

You take something from Beautiful Teacher's desk. It is a stick of waxy stuff used to put paper on the wall. You wait in another classroom for the afternoon bus home and pull out the stick of wax. Another teacher notices you unwrapping it and asks where you got it.

Within a couple of seconds you have the whole story ready as a good Little Con would. You look up at the teacher with clear, innocent eyes. You bat them once and begin.

Your stepfather, not your real daddy who is going to come get you one day, is a scientist and inventor and has a laboratory in the back of your trailer where he, through much thought and lots of hard work, has invented this wonderful thing called stickwax and he gave you some to play with. He is going to sell it and make a lot of money and we will all live happily ever after and have plenty to eat.

The teacher stares, barely concealing her amusement — and worry. She allows you to keep the stick of wax but says to make sure not to bring any more to school because the other children might get upset because they don't have any. You nod gravely — this is the showmanship you're learning to apply when the *mark* falls for the *con* — and tell her with all the earnestness you can put on that you'd hate to make the other children unhappy and you will make sure you never do it again by showing up with the good things in your life.

Not bringing something in does not preclude taking things from fellow students, though. Waiting for the bus another day, you see a girl whose pencils have her name on them. You want a pencil with a name on it. You watch where she puts the pencils. You become invisible and, in front of everybody, take one from her desk. She begins to pack up her stuff to go home. Sitting at a desk across the room, you hear your name called. There's the girl, who thinks you're her friend. She's crying.

Between sobs she explains she lost one of her very expensive pencils with her name on it. She had five and now she has four and Mama's gonna be mad and she's gonna get in trouble and...boo-hoo, boo-hoo. Please, she begs, you're my very best friend, help me find it. Boo-hoo. Boo-hoo.

Two things go through your mind in total opposition to each other.

First: What a sissy girl to cry because she loses one stupid pencil. It's a stupid pencil! She can tell her mother she sharpened it and used it for lots and lots of writing until it was used up. Can't she lie? You can teach her.

Second: This poor girl. She's getting in trouble because you're selfish and bad. You must make this thing right.

Don't worry, you tell her, we will find that pencil right now. It can't have gone far. You say this with such confidence, she smiles as if her pencil was, that very second, restored to her. Look there, you tell her, and let me look here —

You make a big show of thoroughly searching and then aha! Friend, Friend! I found it. Of course, you pretend to find it nowhere near the desk you were in. Girl's head pops up from under a desk. She shrieks in pure happiness as she sees you holding the pencil above your head, and hugs you until you think you'll puke there's so much emotion coming out. You've saved me, she says. You are the best friend ever. Boo-hoo. Boo-hoo.

You untangle yourself, admonish her to take better care of her pencils, and silently vow never again to steal; well, at least you won't steal to satisfy your own selfish longing. You break that vow when you're twelve and steal from a big bag of M&M candies sitting on the kitchen counter of a lady whose car you're cleaning to make money. You had to have those M&Ms and there were so many. You feel bad about that for years and years. When you get the courage up to confess, you can't find her and the guilt remains. Even God can't forgive your evil ways.

Being Little Con wasn't all it was cracked up to be.

Ricky Forsyth

Second grade is momentous. It's the year that, in the class picture, you look like a refugee from a war-torn country. It is also the year you know for a fact God exists, though you still do not know His identity or anything about Him seeing as how Vacation Bible School was such a bust. It happens just before the Christmas season.

Teacher explains to the class there will be this thing called drawing names. Girls draw the names of boys and boys draw the names of girls and whoever's name you draw is the one you buy a Christmas present for. That way, she explains seriously, everybody gets a gift. What a grand idea this is and every child writes their name on a slip of paper and drops it in a hat.

Drawing. Names. A quite interesting pair of words.

You watch as each boy walks to the front of the room, casually reaches in, and opens his drawn slip of paper. Some smile. Some get mad. Some shrug. Some have no expression. The girls want to know who got their names and some time is spent on making those announcements. Then you hear a girl ask Ricky Forsyth whose name he got and hear your name. Your head snaps up. Ricky Forsyth looks at you and smiles. You pray. The girls' drawing turn comes. The prayer is simple and you remember it to this day:

Dear God, let me draw Ricky Forsyth.

Girl draws, giggles, and calls out name of Boy. There is much giggling and groaning as each girl walks to the front, picks, and reads.

Dear God, let me draw Ricky Forsyth.

You repeat this prayer girl after girl, pick after pick. Until you hear your name called. You stand. Finally, you're there. At the hat. You can't breathe. Teacher holds out the hat. You must have Ricky's name. You must have it. Your eyes squeeze shut in one last fervent prayer.

Please, please, dear God, let me draw Ricky Forsyth. Please. Please.

Reach. Pick. You are almost ready to faint. Slip of paper is opened.

Dear God, thank you!

You look at Ricky and he's smiling. You smile back, big, happily, lovingly. God heard and provided what you wanted because He knew what you needed. Happy day. Immediately you know what Ricky Forsyth, the love of your life, will want for a present and only it would do.

He must have a fighter jet airplane model kit because Ricky Forsyth is a real man and he makes you feel great.

When you get home, you find Little Sister also drew the name of a boy in her class and Beloved Mother takes you both shopping for presents. Little Sister doesn't know what to get. You go right to the aisle where the model airplane kits are, zero in on the fighter jets, and pick out the baddest, most fiercest you can find. This involves much comparing and it takes you forever to come to a conclusion. Little Sister finds out what you're doing and decides on a model airplane kit, too, plucking one from the shelf with total nonchalance. She and Beloved Mother whine for you to hurry up and make a choice. They stalk the aisle getting madder and madder.

Normally you'd have hurried through, finished the thing, and kept Beloved Mother and Little Sister calm, though on this you will not be rushed. A man's — Ricky Forsyth's — happiness is at stake, and he is your man and nobody else's, so back off Beloved Mother and Little Sister. They are shocked at the response and shut up and wait until you pick.

Wrapping paper is a must. Beloved Mother asks if you can't just put it in a paper sack and hand it to him, don't you know how much this costs? Your horrified silence must have told her the answer to that silly question and off you all tramp to the aisle with the paper and this thing called tape. Little Sister is glad you insisted on wrapping paper because she wants the fancy stuff, too.

Eventually the planes get wrapped and the day comes to take them to school for the giving. When Ricky Forsyth sees his plane, and how manly and strong it is, then he will know you, and only you, understand him and love him.

Teacher calls for everyone to give presents to their pick. Ricky hands you your present and you hand him his. You both smile shyly. Ricky tears his paper off and —

You want to die.

Stupid Mother gave you the wrong present. You look at Ricky Forsyth. Was your love now dead? He looks at the plane and shouts how did you know what I wanted? He always wanted a model airplane. Always. And now he has one. His expression of pure love as he looks at you makes Beloved Mother's small, minor, tiny mistake become as if it hadn't happened.

Ricky Forsyth is happy and he loves you.

He looks at the still-unwrapped present in your hand. Will you be as happy with it as he is happy with your awesome gift to him? Slowly you peel the tape — hurry, hurry, he says because he wants to see your happiness — and you're stunned. How did he know? How did he know?

He bought you the one thing you never could get enough of: Food.

Rolls and rolls and rolls of Life Savers candy. Every flavor there was in the world and they were all yours.

God exists. Ricky Forsyth loves you. And you made your man happy.

You stare at the twelve rolls and cry. Ricky Forsyth thinks you hate your present and his smile of joy turns to worry. It takes time to convince him it is the most perfect present ever. His worry goes away and he says he's happy you're happy. He walks to his desk, sits, and alternately stares at his plane and you.

Your love is meant to be. You learn another lesson that day, too. Never again will you trust Beloved But Stupid Mother to keep presents straight. Your heart can't handle the pressure.

The Start of Whore

One day you're outside playing at the trailer park and Jimmy Joe Johnson, a boy who lives up the street and is a year older, and whose daddy you danced for, asks if you want to take a walk in the woods. The woods are next to the creek you swing over on a vine. Jimmy Joe spots a nice log and invites you to sit next to him. You do. He smiles.

I'll show you mine if you'll show me yours, he says.

You have no idea what he's talking about. Show me your what? He smiles and says you know. You shake your head that you do not. He looks around, sees no one, stands up, unzips his pants, and pulls out — oh, that. But you don't have one, you tell him, ever logical. He says he knows, but you have something better. He smiles. You stand up and pull your pants down and you stare at each other's parts. Sitting again on the log, the bark bites into your butt and it hurts.

You ignore the pain, though, because you're kinda liking this kissing thing and this being-naked-with-a-boy thing. It's different than the devil-men. Jimmy Joe kisses you and leans back and you notice he is twinkling and you twinkle back to match. Admiration and kissing goes on for a couple of minutes, you both stand, pull up, and zip closed. Hand in hand he walks you back to the trailer and goes home and you smile and smile and feel happy.

Later that evening you're called into the trailer. Honey and Beloved Mother, sitting next to each other on a small sofa, holding hands, are worried about you. It has been reported to them, they intone, that you and Jimmy Joe Johnson were out in the woods together. Is that true? You have nothing to hide on the subject. After all, don't Honey and Beloved Mother and you and all those other men do this stuff all the time? So, you nod a yes.

Honey looks at Beloved Mother. She nods and turns to you. She can't speak and motions for Honey to handle this. Honey turns to you and says what you did with Jimmy Joe out in the woods was wrong, not right, dirty, and only whores do that. Do you want someone to think you are a whore?

You do not know what a whore is, but from their expressions deduce it is not a good thing to be, and shake your head no. Honey says you must confess to him everything that happened with Jimmy Joe. You stand in front of Honey with Beloved Mother sitting at his side, unable to look at you, her head bowed in shame at the wantonness of her daughter, and you tell them everything and there is no smile and no twinkle.

The next day, Jimmy Joe Johnson is mad at you for telling on him. You say you did not tell on him, but were made to confess because otherwise you would be a whore and you don't want to be a whore. Jimmy Joe gets mad and says you aren't a whore and what you did was nothing wrong and certainly not any worse than —

He stops. Worse than what, you ask? Nothing, he says, and walks away never to talk to you again. You think of his twinkle and your short-lived happiness and you cannot, for the life of you, figure out what was wrong with what you two did.

Being analytical and always trying to figure out the adults in your life, you begin to compare what you did with Jimmy Joe with what you do with Devil. You liked what you did with Jimmy Joe. You liked Jimmy Joe. You didn't like what you did with Devil. You hated Devil and loved Honey. If doing what you did with Jimmy Joe could make you a whore, whatever that was, then you must really be worse than a whore because you did a whole lot more with Devil and his friends.

Then you hear your name called. It's Weak Mother at the front door of the trailer. You know from her tone what you must now do. You have to be a whore for Devil. You don't want to be a whore for Devil. You don't like the taste and always throw up afterward. But you walk into the bedroom into which Beloved Mother has called you. Devil's lying on the bed. He's naked. He's looking at you. You stand at the foot of the bed and look from Devil to Weak Mother. You say you don't want to do this anymore and can't you just not do it?

Devil gets mad. Beloved But Weak Mother stands at the head of the bed and tells you to please do this thing — now! — so she won't get beat. You stare at Weak Mother, climb on the bed, and the next thing you remember is throwing up in the bathroom. It takes some time to finish throwing up, then you're allowed to go outside and play.

A high school boy from across the street sees you come out of the trailer and walks over. He says it was him who told on you and Jimmy Joe. He says he doesn't want you to become a bad girl. You stare, saying nothing, then run to where playing is going on, your mouth and throat still burning from whoring and puking.

You vowed you'd find a way not to be a bad girl because you knew you weren't a bad girl even though everybody else seemed to be pushing you that way — and God heard...

God Hears...Sort of

Around this time Grandmother visits. She seems very anxious to talk to you privately. She needn't have worried about anyone else being around because they couldn't have understood the conversation anyway because it was about God. Grandmother brings three books that, she says, are wonderful, and she wants you to have them and read them. They will explain all about God and The End Times and will be very helpful. You're not sure how Grandmother knows you need to learn about God, but she does.

You're surprised God can be learned about from books. You take the books and hold them. One cover is green and another is red and the titles hint at the knowledge within. You open the red one and see a picture of what is obviously a drunken whore. She even has a name: Babylon the Great. Was this what people thought you were? The picture is so terrible you do not open the

books again for years, but keep them because they are about God and, besides, Grandmother gave them to you.

Grandmother didn't stay long; after all, she had a lot of friends to visit and had to get on down the road. So she did, but only after pointedly telling you to read the books. Read them, girl. You nod yes.

Twinkling for Profit, or Becoming a Playboy Bunny

Every time you go to a new school, a teacher always asks what you want to be when you grow up. Your answer is always the same: A teacher.

The teachers smile and say wonderful and then they say you'd make a great teacher and blah, blah, blah, because by now you've tuned them out. Why? Because you already know what you're going to be when you grow up and it definitely isn't a teacher.

Devil decreed you would become the most famous, most respected, and most highly paid whore in the world: A Playboy Bunny. He never called the Playboy Bunnies whores, but you knew that's what they were because they get naked for men to look at and they twinkle and men say things about them they say about you and since you know you're a whore and can twinkle, then they had to be whores too.

Becoming a Playboy Bunny will make you a respectable whore. The grooming for your life's work begins like this: Next to Honey's naugahyde easy chair that somehow manages to follow from town to town no matter how fast the law is after him, is a pile of magazines Devil keeps. You are encouraged to look through them anytime and you do. Some feature Playboy Bunnies and cartoons with Santa delivering big gifts and ladies shopping for fruit, so how bad could these magazines be?

Other magazines have pictures of women getting beat. Oh, so other Beloved Mothers have the same problem. Interesting. Some have pictures of women beating men. And dog leashes and whips. These you do not understand. Other magazines have pictures of things you have no knowledge of and nothing to compare them to, so you never understand them either.

Often Devil sits you in his lap and together you flip through the magazines, open to the centerfold, and talk about the fine points or shortcomings of each of the women. Devil explains you have to be better than these in order to get in *this* magazine.

So when teachers ask what you're going to be when you grow up, you've already learned they don't really want to know the truth about your life and you never tell them you will be a Playboy Bunny. You hate lying, but what can you do? So you continue saying you're gonna be a teacher.

There came a point, though, when a decision was made not to do these things Devil wanted; he was not happy. But that's a few years later.

Obsession

You fell in love. You never knew his name; he was in another class, but on the playground you got two other girls to help you. The three of you chased him; they held his arms and legs while you kissed him over and over again. He screamed and screamed, indignant that a girl was kissing him and Teacher said to let him go. You laid another big fat one on him and told the girls to let him up. He got madder when his friends laughed.

The next day, and for several days after that, you repeated your campaign, catching him far away from the teachers. They didn't hear his screams, or if they did they couldn't see his situation and a little kid screaming on the playground somewhere is not to be paid attention to. Your two friends thought you were so brave to kiss a boy. Heck, kissing a boy is easy, you tell them, bragging.

Finally, two teachers find out about the campaign and explain it isn't right to hold somebody against their will and do those things to them. It is wrong. You don't comprehend and have to think about it.

Wrong to hold someone against their will?

Could it be Devil and Weak Mother were wrong? You didn't say it out loud, of course, because by now you know never to open your mouth about what happens at home, but according to Teacher they are very wrong. Is Teacher right? You hope so.

You still loved The Boy In The Other Classroom, as you named him. Somehow you manage to wait for the bus in his classroom. His mother picked him up every day and he isn't there waiting with you, but you find out which desk is his and make sure you sit in it every day. You know it's his cute little butt that sat where your little butt is now. You go through his desk, learning everything you can about him.

And you leave a simple, unsigned note where he will find it the next day when he goes into his desk.

I love you.

The next day: I love you very much.

The next day: I love you very, very much.

Each day you add one more very to the perfectly punctuated and accurately spelled and always unsigned note until there are fifteen verys.

You get near him on the playground — you can do that without him seeing because you know how to be invisible — and hear him telling his buddies about the notes. He has each one and he's furious. Mostly, he's scared. You know he's scared because you know what scared looks like. He says he doesn't understand why the notes are unsigned. The other boys throw out girls' names one after the other, and he shakes his head and says he just doesn't know. No one ever throws out your obvious perfectly-fitting-to-the-situation name.

Conclusion: Boys are so stupid.

Still, you don't want The Boy In The Other Classroom to be scared, so that day, at great personal sacrifice, you stop the notes and do not sit at his desk ever again even though your little butt so wants to be close to his little butt. And you pine for him and miss him and want him, but you can't bring yourself to scare him anymore and somehow you know he would not like you anyway, Whore

Jealousy and Satisfaction

Beautiful Teacher knows Honey!

The shock you feel upon seeing Honey talking with Beautiful Teacher is not welcome. Beautiful Teacher is an artist and so is Honey and they're talking about oil painting and such as that while you stand in front of an easel in an art class with ten other kids, all of whom can draw and paint better. You try hard to draw the apples and grapes in the bowl so that Honey will be proud and pay attention to you instead of Beautiful Teacher.

But your sketch is terrible and you want to rip it off the easel and tear it up, destroy it, before anyone sees the less-than-perfect work. Honey says you'll get better and one day you'll be an artist, too. You know he's wrong because, while you understand words, this drawing thing does not make any sense at all. You look up at Honey and try to twinkle, but can't. Honey senses your troubles and puts his arm around your shoulders and actually comforts you and you feel safe and loved as you walk out to the car to go home.

At school, Beautiful Teacher said y'all will make a special art project everyone would be good at and each one will look beautiful. She passes out big white sheets of paper. She says take a black crayon and make this mark and that mark — and y'all do. Before long everyone has a pattern of varying shapes all connected in a crazy pattern. Here comes the fun part, she says. Put your favorite color inside the shapes, some light, some heavy, and see what happens.

Students eagerly pick their favorites and fall to filling in the shapes. Beautiful Teacher walks around the room, stopping at each desk and exclaiming about the good job and the beautiful colors. She gets to your desk and stares. She says nothing and you keep coloring intently.

The job of coloring was excellent, by the way. Compulsive obsession was already in play even then. There was no coloring outside the lines. Each shade was within its own borders and every shape had its own shade. No two were repeated. It was beautiful. Then you heard the question.

Did you hear me say to pick your favorite color?

You stop coloring and look up at Beautiful Teacher. She does not look unhappy; more worried than anything else. You nod: Yes, indeed you heard her say just that. So why didn't you pick your favorite color? When you tell her black is your favorite color, she doesn't know what to say. Finally, she pats your shoulder, nods, and goes to the next desk. You bend to finish your beautiful picture. You begin to understand this drawing thing. Beautiful Teacher is very smart to help. The satisfaction you feel when it is done lasts several days.

Satisfaction. Not a word you understood, but you liked this new feeling of being full mentally and emotionally to the point of sensory overload. You liked it a lot and began looking for opportunities to get that feeling again and again.

Aversion Therapy

Yes, your time at the trailer park is weird, as the second-grade picture attests. Still, one thing happens that is beneficial; Devil — Honey? Devil? Honey-Devil? — made it happen.

Little Sister loved to bite. Let her get mad and she would be sneaking up and biting the ever-living fire out of you.

So there you are, quietly screaming again in pain you didn't see coming so you didn't have time to prepare for it, in the back of the car, going down Georgia Highway 85, trying to pry the Jaws of Death off your arm once again and having a devil of a time doing it because her hands are wrapped around it as she squeezes and bites like it's a cob of corn.

Devil's driving and Little Baby Brother sees what's happening and, sweetie pie that he is and young as he is and not understanding the nature of your quiet scream, jumps right to Daddy and says something and points and Devil goes absolutely ballistic.

He screams, reaches over the back of the seat, grabs Little Sister by the arm and hauls until she's laying upside down over the back of the seat and he's cussing her and she's fighting and he says he's gonna teach her a goddamned lesson about biting and —

Little Sister screams bloody murder and you jump up in the back seat to get a better view and see Honey-Devil with her arm between his teeth and he's giving it all he's got with what teeth he has remaining and you go down the highway like that for what seems ages.

He drops her into the back of the car and she hits the floor sobbing in pain, clutching her arm, and Honey-Devil says she better not bite Big Sister again because if she does she's really gonna get it.

Miracle of miracles: She never bites again. It wasn't the first nor the last time Little Sister had to learn a lesson the hard way.

That is your first memory of someone protecting you and you like that feeling. It will not happen often enough to ever get used to it. Lots of men will make offers and promises to help, to protect, to always be there, whatever that means. Just call me, they say, and you decide to believe.

You believe the first one until you need some little thing and it isn't convenient. You believe the second one until you need some small favor that can't be done for whatever reason. And so as men continue to open their wellmeaning mouths to make promises that make them feel good, little by little you believe them less and less until one day you want to tell them they are full of shit but don't.

When they ask if you believe them, you always say of course, though you don't, but the smile is there and they believe you believe.

Old habits die hard.

Killing Turtle

During the summer between first and second grade, a little boy who lived on the other side of the trailer park ran out of the woods screaming he found a giant turtle and everyone should come see. Of course, fifteen kids had to see and off they took to the woods, across the creek, and up the hill. And there it was. The biggest turtle you ever saw.

The boy said he was going to kill it and who wanted to help? He picks up the turtle and slams it to the ground. He does it again. Another boy joins in. Slam. Slam. Slam.

You see the turtle at first is mad, then he's scared, then he's hurting. You don't want the turtle to hurt anymore. You tell the boy you want a turn and all the little girls are horrified. You pick it up and slam it to the ground hard, and that's really hard because you're strong. Screaming, you egg on the boys and continue to take your turn — fast, fast, faster, kill the turtle.

Soon, Turtle's broken into pieces, his insides spread everywhere. His hard shell had not saved him, but was the challenge the boys needed. Turtle is out of pain now and you're happy for Turtle. You stare at him one last time and walk back home without saying a word. That gets put in the back of your mind in a box and shut in.

You thought you forgot about Turtle until three things happen when you're a new driver and memories come flooding back bigger than death itself in eight or nine years or so; what it costs you to kill something you will only find out then.

Goose it, Honey

One of the things you very much adored about Honey was he loved to go fast, and you couldn't get enough of speed. The first time you remember going very fast, you were in second grade; it was in the ragtop convertible that was the family car. Honey told you to climb in and off you went on a mini date.

On your knees on the front seat by Honey, holding on to the back of the seat with one hand and bracing yourself on the dash with the other. He hit the gas. Up the hill, over the speed breakers, and out onto Georgia Highway 85 that ran in front of the trailer park. Windows down, long hair whipping around your head, and you had to keep shaking it out of your eyes. The world speeding by and you must see the blur of it.

He screeches to a halt on the highway, turns and asks if you want to do something more fun. You scream yes. He smiles, puts it in reverse, and guns it again. You look out the back window, feeling fear of the backward motion yet happiness in the speed mixed with wonderment that no other cars were hitting you. How they ever managed to avoid crashing you never did figure out, but they did; years later you remember their screaming faces as they whipped around the two screaming nuts going backward on the narrow two-lane.

Honey screeches to a halt again. You look at each other. You, panting in excitement, fueled his desire to please a woman. You screamed at him to goose it, Honey, goose it! And off you went again, this time forward. He screamed over the wind and told you to guess how fast the car was going. You, who knew numbers because you were in second grade, looked at the needle and screamed one-hundred-and-twenty-five!

You heard Honey say uh-oh and he whipped into the trailer park, hit the speed breakers hard, and slung the car into its spot in front of the trailer. You both jump out, slam car doors, and run inside to tell Beloved Mother. She turns to Honey and says something you don't remember, but she isn't happy, and he tells her to stop ruining all his fun.

Then he turns to you again and you talk and talk and talk about it. You twinkle mightily, but this time it's because you're so happy. Happier than you'd ever been and you loved Honey because he went fast and he understood your need for the speed and he didn't want to take your fun away this time by bringing out Devil.

Come Out With Your Hands Up

Devil was a bad man. In prison fourteen years. Jumped parole. Knifed people. Sold drugs. Got in fights. Shot twice in the gut. Killed his sister. Used drugs. Got drunk. Loved up on you. Beat Beloved Mother and Little Sister and Baby Brothers. Played dirty tricks on people. Drove his car very, very fast. Wanted by police in several states.

He was also getting tired of running. Devil, twenty-five years older than Beloved Mother, and now over fifty, is tired of always looking over his shoulder. You had been living in the trailer for a while, the one Grandfather bought when the family stopped hiding out in Florida, and now you're in second grade when Devil gets the bright idea he should turn himself in to the police.

He leaves and in a couple of hours he's back, shaking his head in wonder at their stupidity. You hear him tell Beloved Mother and several neighbors all about how he went to the station, told them about his wanted state, told them to look it up and make a call, and they laughed and said for him to take his old self on back home. Stop causing them grief, they chided the old man, we have real bad guys to worry about.

The neighbors laugh. Beloved Mother smiles. And you go about playing in the yard casually digging yet another hole to China.

A couple of hours later sirens are wailing and getting closer. They're coming down the street, over the speed breakers, and screech into your yard, not far from where you're digging with Little Sister and Baby Brothers. Baby Brothers never look up and the hole gets bigger. Little Sister and you pause to look between digs. Car doors fly open, policemen stand behind them, draw their guns, cock them, point them toward the front door of the trailer, and a badge man holding this thing that makes his voice very loud hollers come out with your hands up.

Come out with your hands up echoes with the sirens against the trailers and the woods and you cock your head and listen. Interesting. You make a note to remember that sound, how it bounced around, then you fall to digging again, pause, look, dig, look.

You see Beloved Mother open the door and say don't shoot, he's coming. She steps down and moves to the side and there is Devil, standing in the door, framed in the sunlight, hands up, shaking his head and smiling and saying in a loud voice I told you so. You hear shut up and get down and see Devil lying on the ground and policemen advancing on him with guns drawn and then he is in handcuffs and jerked upright and thrown into the back of a police car and you and Little Sister keep digging, watching the show between little shovels full of slung dirt, slowly making a passage to China where the people with eyes that slant live. But do they slant up or down? You never can remember. You hum the little tune you know.

Chinese. Japanese. American knees.

Slant up or slant down? Up or down? Oh, well. You'll find out when you get there. But, how do American knees slant?

Devil smiles at you from the back of the police car and you smile back confidently and wave bye-bye and get busy digging again. You aren't worried for Devil. Don't they know they can't hurt him because he is Devil and he is strong?

He'll be back, but only after Grandfather posts a ten-thousand-dollar bail because Beloved Mother begs her daddy who never left her to get her man out of jail, and Devil comes back just like you knew he would. He is on parole in Georgia for the next few years. When you go to New York to visit his relatives, he does not get permission from his parole officer. Second grade ends and you leave the trailer park and move. Yeah, he just couldn't stop being a bad man and you leave trouble behind again.

Dancing Princess

Dancing has always been in your life. You danced to save Little Sister. You danced for the devil-men. You danced as you stomped glass balls. You danced to save Snake.

Then one day you began to dance for yourself — and it drove Devil crazy. It started at the end of second grade.

If music played, you danced. It didn't matter where. In your head? Dance. Band in a parking lot festival? Dance. School assembly? Dance. Back seat of the car? Dance. Grocery store? Gas station? Kmart? Street? Hardware store? Dance, dance, dance. Sitting, your feet bounce and your hands wave in time. Walking, you twirl and leap and pirouette and are the most graceful ballerina in the whole wide world. New shoes? You are a tap dancer and stomp happily in time to whatever music there is wherever you find it.

It fills your heart and mind with joy and you need your heart and mind filled with something good.

One day, while shopping in Kmart, you hear Honey say to Beloved Mother: Can't you get her to goddamn stop? She's driving me crazy. I can't take it anymore.

Honey walks down the aisle and Beloved Mother comes to tell you to stop. Stop what? She says dancing. You say you can't. She begs and you can't stop. Honey stares down the aisle and then says to just keep her away from him while she's dancing.

You didn't understand that because he liked you to dance for him and devil-men. That was confusing, but still you didn't stop; you couldn't stop.

Donning Gay Apparel

At the start of third grade, when the family again moved away from trouble, you began what would become a lifelong habit: Quickly exploring the greater world around where you now live. If the huge, fancy churches are any indication, God is much in evidence in this little town and you still hadn't found out much about Him yet.

One Sunday morning during the early fall, you feel an overpowering need for God and think you'll give one of these fancy churches a try. You reason out that Vacation Bible School didn't work so well in informing you about God because the church had been small. Surely God is in one of these big churches.

But what to wear? A fancy church calls for fancy clothes and you have none. You remember the two fancy things you have, gifts from Devil. But not one of your dresses is fancy enough.

You go into Beloved Mother's closet because she gets dressed up a lot when she and Devil go out; she had some nice things. After rejecting several items for various reasons —wrong color, not fancy enough, and so forth — you find two items that work perfectly. You're almost giddy as you run to your room.

Outfit complete, you take off by yourself out the front door. Which church will you go to? Where is God most likely to be found? That was still an open question, but you knew you'd figure it out. Down the sidewalk. Across the railroad tracks. Wait for the light to change. Green for go, red for stop, be your own little traffic cop. Don't cross the street until you see the traffic light has turned to green. Down the next sidewalk.

You didn't like the first church and bypassed it. But the next one, oh wow. The next one had a steeple that went way high. And it looked like a temple in Greece you saw once in a book, huge white columns and three giant sets of doors in the front. Surely God was here more than any other place.

Your feet turned from the sidewalk to the pavement in front of the steps. You didn't casually walk up. No, that would not do. You approached the entrance to God solemn, ready to hear. You knew you were approaching properly, not just casually walking, because all the people stopped and stared as you walked into the church.

What did the people see and make a path for?

They saw a third-grade girl, blonde, green eyes, serious, holding herself straight and tall, plastic diamond tiara on her head, high-heeled purple princess shoes on her feet, a crinoline tucked high under her armpits so it wouldn't drag the ground, topped with a beautiful fur jacket hanging to her knees, honoring God with the finest she could dredge up.

The next thing you remember, you're walking into the house and Honey is bent over laughing while Beloved Mother demands to know what you're doing dressed in her clothes. You calmly reply you've been searching for God at the church down the street. Honey stops laughing and looks at you with a seriousness never before seen in him. Beloved Mother shakes her head and looks at you like she always does: Who are you and where did you come from?

She wants her clothes back. Now.

The Sad Day

Little-girl wishes are mighty powerful. And your wishes for Daddy to come get you are no less so. Every time things got worse than bad you would think Daddy's gonna come get me. But he didn't and one day when things were worse than bad and you brought out your wish for Daddy to help you through, you stopped making that wish, and never made it again.

You remember clearly the thought process. Why wish for something that is never going to happen when you aren't gonna get it? The disappointment is too big. Why set yourself up for more?

So the dream of Daddy died when you were in second grade. That was a very, very sad day. When a little girl can't count on her own daddy to save her, who can she count on? Nobody, that's who; nobody except herself. So Daddy ceased to exist and you never thought of him again.

Never again, that is, until third grade when you lived in the town of the big churches and Beloved Mother came in and said your suitcase was packed and Daddy would be there any minute to pick up you and Little Sister and take you to visit your other grandfather and grandmother you did not even know were alive. You didn't know you had a suitcase, either.

So here comes Missing Daddy. You didn't know what he looked like and now here was this tall man, smiling and laughing, and he looked handsome, too. You didn't smile; Little Sister ran to him and he picked her up. He said hello to you very gravely and the four of you walked to the car. It was four because he had another wife, though you didn't know that was what this woman was. She got to sit in the front seat by Daddy and you were told to sit in back. But this is *Daddy*. She gave you a dirty look upon that pronouncement, and the car took off. You did not wave to Beloved Mother.

You weren't sure what to do about this situation because Daddy ceased to be once you stopped wishing for him to come and now here he was. The trip to Rome, where his parents lived, was long and hard. Finally you make it and Daddy stops at a drugstore and lets you and Little Sister go in with him. He tells you to pick a toy and he'll buy it.

You pick the most expensive toy, but price wasn't why you picked it.

You picked it because it was a bubble gum machine and you wanted a bubble gum machine and Daddy said to pick a toy. When he pointed out it was the most expensive, you didn't understand. Hadn't he said to pick a toy?

Yes, he had, he said.

So you did and now he doesn't want to buy it?

No, that's not what I mean, he says; you get the bubble gum machine because he never came all those times you wished for him. His wife is furious about spending money on the little brats and he tells her to shut up and out you walk to go spend time with the grandparents you never knew you had.

Lots of relatives are there and you remember playing with a bunch of kids you later find out are cousins and everybody keeps saying how pretty you are, but you never once twinkle on the entire trip. You never twinkle because you're furious at that woman for not letting you have Daddy. She hogs him for herself and keeps you away. Go play, she says. Leave us alone, she says. You don't have the right to come in here, she says.

The days pass and then you're home and the suitcase comes out of the car with the bubble gum machine and you are not happy to see Beloved Mother or Honey or Baby Brothers. You couldn't have generated a one-watt twinkle if your life or anybody else's depended on it. You vaguely remember saying goodbye and you didn't wave when Daddy and that woman left.

And then the dream of Daddy was truly dead because he hadn't waved goodbye either. You'd see him four more times. Once when you're thirteen and he's passing through and Beloved Mother takes him to the airport after he visits for a few minutes and she comes home saying he wanted to fornicate with her but she wouldn't because she is a good Christian woman and he laughed and said yeah, right, he knew what she was like with that and you, now in seventh grade, wonder why she tells you this stuff.

Once when you were in your mid-twenties and saw him at a family reunion. Once more in your late twenties when he visited your home during a trip. And the last time at his funeral.

He never waved goodbye then either.

Devil and Police Chief

In third grade you live in a large house two blocks away from the courthouse and jail. Devil's been gone for two months, though he isn't dying this time; he's locked up in jail. The day arrives for his release and you come home from school to find him sitting in his naugahyde chair, pushed back flat as far as possible, and he's gripping the armrests tight. Beloved Mother goes to work and leaves you and Little Sister to wash the dinner dishes.

You're not happy about this chore and one by one, piece by piece, you take plates, forks, cups, and walk over to Honey and ask what to do with this thing. Honey looks at each piece and says: Wash it. Finally you bring him the big pot full of the rest of dinner that didn't get eaten and frankly, even with your usual hunger, was so bad you don't want to save it. By this time he is frustrated and says to take the pot full of the goddamned food and walk it up to the goddamned police chief.

You walk slowly back into the dining room. Put the pot on the table, put the lid on the pot, walk up to your bedroom, get your coat, walk down the stairs into the dining room, pick up the pot, and head out the back door. You're almost to the jail when you hear running and someone screaming stop, stop, stop. It's Honey. You've never seen him move so fast. He gets to you and asks where in the hell do you think you're going? You reply: The jail. Honey asks if you hate him and want him back in jail. You prudently do not answer the truth and shake your head no.

He asks why you're taking the pot to the jail. You reply: Because he told you to. He gently takes the pot and you walk back to the house where Little Sister is washing dishes.

That is, she is supposed to be washing dishes. Instead she stands on a stool in front of the sink and pitches royal fits in this way: Wash a fork, stomp her feet, scream, cry, rinse the fork, scratch her leg, and holler why can't Big Sister do this, it isn't fair. You give Honey credit for using as much self-control as he does. After two hours of her fits and him continually begging her to shut the fuck up, he can't take it anymore. Do you want to get beat, he asks her.

He knows there's something wrong with her, she must be just a little bit touched in the head, and he knows this because she won't stop and eggs him on until finally — you're watching this with glee — he storms into the kitchen as he pulls off his belt, and begins to beat her. He holds an arm. She screams and dances in a circle. He's beating her butt, at least he's aiming at her butt; she keeps jumping around and gets hit everywhere. He's begging her the whole time to please just fucking stop so he can hit her butt. She won't. And you don't want her to stop. You want her to be beat because she beats you all the time and you let her because she is a lot touched.

Finally, finally, finally she takes a deep breath, shudders, and is fine. She steps to the sink to finish the dishes and you look at Honey. He is breathing deeply, worn out from the effort, overwhelmed from dealing with her, and doesn't see you because you've become invisible so you can watch this beating.

And you know Little Sister needs it. This happens several times during the years. Honey, not Devil, will beg her to please stop her fit. She won't. She'll torture him until he can't take it anymore and he'll beat her until she shudders and becomes as normal as Little Sister can be.

She still beats you, though. Until one day when you can't take it anymore and tell her to stop — but that takes a few more years.

The Diner and the Five-and-Dime

Exploration of the new big-church town continues. You live right next to the railroad tracks in a huge two-story home with a basement where the coal truck can dump through a little door, and two blocks down from the courthouse and jail. Across the tracks is Main Street. You must walk down Main Street every day to get to school.

By now you look for money anywhere you can find it. Coin on the ground? It's yours; you squirrel it without telling anyone except Little Sister. She keeps her mouth shut, too, because she knows you're going to spend the money on candy to share with her. She might be crazy, but she ain't stupid.

Each day you walk by this thing called a diner. Through the big windows in the front you see men sitting on stools in front of a high counter and want to sit there with them. You tell Little Sister to come in with you and sit at the counter. Little Sister refuses day after day and the trek to school continues.

The day comes when you must sit at that counter with these people doing this mysterious thing, watching the woman behind the counter as she walks fast back and forth, back and forth. What is she doing? What are they doing? You must know now.

You tell Little Sister you're going in, even though you're scared to death, and you want her with you because when she is there you are always braver. She won't come. She stamps her feet, jerks her hand out of yours, and says no. Then she throws down a challenge when she says you're too scared to go in and you won't so let's just go on to school.

The challenge has been issued and you are not scared you say and she says oh yes you are and you say oh yeah, just watch, and you turn around, open the door, hear a bell tinkle and look up at it, let the door close and take two more steps, then look back at Little Sister whose nose is pressed against the glass and whose eyes are big and whose mouth is opened in a big wide O of horror as she watches Big Sister do this brave thing.

A man smiles at you. You nod as if you belong. At the counter one stool is empty. You walk over like you own the place. You climb up. It's way high, too, but you make it. You sit. All the men look at you. This you're used to and now feel confident. The fast-walking woman stops and asks what you want. You say you will have a glass of water because everyone else has a glass of water sitting next to their coffee cup and since you aren't allowed to drink coffee or soft drinks, water it is.

The men smile and eat again, glancing occasionally at you; fast-walking woman sets a glass of water down in front of you. You thank her and drink the water. You slide down off the stool, open the door but don't look up at the little tinkle, and walk out. Little Sister peels herself off the window. You take her hand and continue on to school.

This is repeated for several mornings with Little Sister always watching from the street, no longer horrified but in complete awe of Big Sister's bravery. Yes, you repeat it until one morning the fast-walking lady says the glass of water will cost five cents. Several men give her a dirty look, though they don't offer to pay when you say you don't have five cents for a glass of water; after all, candy must be bought. You slide down and never return.

So the next place on Main Street you begin haunting is the five-anddime. Such treasures you did not know existed. It is in this place you find things for a penny. One of those is candy. At the counter is a display with Hershey's Kisses — you love Hershey's Kisses — that can be bought two for a penny. For days on end after school, you and Little Sister stop in, go through every bin for the latest interesting thing and discuss each at great length. Then you go to the counter and each buy two chocolate kisses for a penny.

Until one day you aren't wanting two kisses. You only want one and you want your change from the penny. The man says there is nothing smaller than a penny and you must take the second kiss. You do not want the second kiss but you do want your change. You say to him it isn't right you should pay one penny for one kiss when two kisses can be had for one penny. So you want what's owed you. The man says to give the other kiss to your sister. Little Sister doesn't want but two and she's already got hers, she shakes her head no, so what's he gonna do about it?

He looks over the counter. He has the same expression Beloved Mother gets when she doesn't know what to do with you either. On this point you will not be swayed. You want your change and want it now. The conversation — rather, the debate — goes on for quite some time until finally he asks if you'd be willing to take the second kiss tomorrow.

So, you say, you will pay him today for both kisses, you will eat one today, and tomorrow you will come in and eat the other. Is that correct? He nods his head gravely. But, will he remember he owes you a kiss? He says he will remember. You will not try to cheat me, you ask. He promises and crosses his heart and hopes to die and will stick a needle in his eye if he lies. You stare at him a while longer, and make the decision to believe him. You nod, give him the penny, and take one kiss. You stand there and eat it and you and Little Sister leave for home.

The next day when you arrive, you say nothing and walk up to the counter; he sees you and points to the kisses. You pick up one and show him that, yes indeed, per your agreement you have one kiss, which you unwrap in front of him and eat. Your first long-term financial transaction is done.

A Girl Spends the Night

Halfway through third grade, you move from the city of the big churches to another Main Street where you live on a huge lot with two huge houses, one of which you live in and the other in which Beloved Mother rents out rooms. To the left of the lot is a Burger King. Once a week you get to choose either a hot dog or this new thing called a Whopper. It is a very hard decision and you begin thinking about it at least two days ahead of time.

To the right is an A&P Grocery. You take Baby Brothers' red wagon and walk up and down the streets picking up soft drink bottles and bring them to this store and get the deposit money, which you squirrel away without telling anyone except Little Sister.

Down from you on Main Street is Marie's Gift Shop — she has great Grab Bags; the Feed and Seed — they sell baby yellow chickens at Easter; a sign painter you stop in and watch — silently; a hardware store — where you will buy a mini bike when you're in fifth grade for your second long-term financial transaction; a piano store — you'll visit one day with Honey; and some other stores you don't need to remember so you don't.

One day a little girl shows up at the house. You vaguely remember her from the town of the big churches. She reminds you she lived around the corner. She brings a stack of 45-rpm records, all the latest tunes, and she is spending the night. A girl spending the night has never happened before, but she's a guest and so you figure you need to make her feel at home which means you need to make sure she feels safe because, after all, she is at Devil's house and you must twinkle with all your might so Devil will never notice her. And you do.

You twinkle when the records are played and twinkle when you dance to those records and twinkle at supper and twinkle that evening when it comes time for your occasional evening ritual — the ritual Devil has decided will take place on this most special night.

So there you all are, Devil sitting back in his naugahyde chair holding a Camel unfiltered you light for him in Playboy Bunny fashion, Girl Guest, Beloved Mother, Little Sister, and Baby Brothers. The television is on and the 45s are playing. Devil nods and you take off your clothes. Girl Guest is shocked and wants to know what you're doing.

You assure her this is normal. After all, you tell her, when God created Adam and Eve, He created them naked. This you learned from Devil, the Atheist. People should not be ashamed of their nakedness, you're not, and you finish undressing. You encourage her to take off her clothes and dance with you, but only if she feels like it; after all, she is a guest.

She disappears and you dance and twinkle assuming she will be back shortly. A loud knock comes at the door. Who could it be this late? The police? Everyone gets still and looks at each other. Beloved Mother gets up to answer the door. You stop dancing naked and only stand there naked as the door opens.

It is a man and a woman. The man is furious, the woman is scared, and both are shocked seeing you standing there with no clothes on, looking at them. Girl Guest screams — oh, there she is — and runs from the hall. They grab her and disappear into the night. The screen door slams shut, Beloved Mother closes the front door, Devil turns to you. You twinkle and dance.

You ask Beloved Mother a few days later when Girl Guest will come get her 45s. She says Girl Guest will never be back and the records are yours to keep.

Other Devil-Men

For the most part, you try not to remember the faces of the other devil-men Devil brings into your life. They come, they go, mostly because Devil keeps moving one step ahead of the law. Even though he tries to get himself straight with the law and turn himself in and goes on parole when you're in second grade, he still manages to be the bad boy wherever he goes. This often necessitates moving quickly, no forewarning, changing schools, and always being the new kid everywhere.

There are two devil-men you remember. One rents a room in the big house next door and is the daddy of a little girl and a little boy; they only visit once. This devil-man dresses in suits and wears ties; his hair is always slicked back and he is always, always smiling. The other is a policeman who brings cookies because he knows what you like and he knows what you will do for a cookie. It's a good cookie, too.

Suited Devil likes you. You know this because at your one and only birthday party, he brings you a gift — an umbrella. You wait for him to hand you the gift as others present their gifts. He sits on a chair. He says for you to come get this present. You sidle up to him trying to stay out of arm's reach because you don't like him. He keeps the umbrella close to him and you're forced — you want that umbrella! — to get close. He gently clasps his hand around your arm and slowly pulls you to him. He picks you up and puts you on his lap.

In front of everybody, he wiggles you on his lap, a lap that is poking you and you know what that hard thing is. Devil is watching this new devil-man closely. He sees you don't like him, but Devil doesn't know what to do. Beloved Mother forces a smile as she waits for a twinkle about your umbrella.

You turn to Suited Devil and twinkle and say thank you and pretend to be excited and manage to get out of his lap even as he asks where you're going and you pretend not to hear as you run to play with your guests. You're not sure when he leaves because by now you are engrossed in the party games.

Because you are so good at sports, these party games are easy and you win each one. Beloved Mother, in front of all the guests, says you aren't allowed to win the games at your own party. You ask why then even play? With a little stomp of emphasis, she says to let others win. You say let them win on their own by being better. She gets mad and demands you lose on purpose.

This you cannot do and you pitch a fit. You stomp your foot and tell her that it is unacceptable to lose on purpose and let someone else win. Doesn't that mean it really isn't a loss and really isn't a win if everybody is pretending? Beloved Mother insists and the argument continues while all the guests wait to drop clothespins through the narrow neck of a milk jug.

Honey saves the day. He comes over and gently puts his arms around you and pulls you close while telling Beloved Mother to continue with the games, and he takes you to another room. He says that you're correct. It is a shitty thing to have to lose on purpose, but sometimes you have to make others feel good because they are guests, and then they will love you. If that means pretending to lose and making like you're happy losing, then you do it, and you can't let them know you're losing on purpose.

He tells you to save your talents for playing the games at school and he'll teach you some games one day that you will be very good at and won't have to lose when you play the pool sharks and ping-pong experts. You do not know these games. True to his word, he teaches you a couple of years later.

Anyway, this you understand from Honey and the party ends successfully; you have your umbrella, and Beloved Mother cleans up.

During the night not long after this party, you're awakened when the door to your room on the second floor slowly, quietly opens. The silhouette now closing the door is not Devil. You know who it is. Suited Devil has managed to sneak into the house, up the stairs, and is now coming for you.

Just as he reaches the bed and is pulling the covers back, the door opens in a quiet, controlled burst. They fight silently. Suited Devil grunts as Honey punches. Suited Devil makes the same mistake a lot of people make about Honey; they think because he is smaller that he is weak. He is very strong, as tall and broad and handsome Suited Devil soon learns. You hear the struggle quietly taken out the door, down the hall, down the stairs, and hear the back door open and slam shut.

You hear Honey's soft footsteps as he makes his way back to your room. You pretend you're asleep and didn't see anything; he makes sure you're covered up, and closes the door quietly when he leaves. And you are grateful to be saved by the Devil. Who, by the way, never mentions Suited Devil again, nor does he say anything about what happened that night. You find a tool that says it will cut glass and go over to the house next door where Suited Devil has rented the lower apartment and when no one is looking you take that tool and try to cut every window in his place. The tool doesn't work and even though you press hard, the glass doesn't cut. You see these little scratches and so content yourself with making a lot of scratches all over his windows in pretty patterns.

The next day you see a crowd around Suited Devil's apartment. The women's arms are crossed as they stare and the men scratch their heads as they try to decipher why Suited Devil broke all his windows.

Suited Devil insists all he did was open the windows to let in a breeze and when he closed them, each and every one shattered. No one believes him, and he's told he must pay for the repair of every huge window. He continues to protest his innocence; Honey stares, eyes cold and full of promise of telling dark secrets if he doesn't pay. Suited Devil isn't stupid and agrees.

You find out later Suited Devil killed himself when his wife reported him to the police for being a devil with his son. He had been a devil with his daughter first, but the wife never reported that. So he killed himself and you were happy he was gone.

Police Devil you're introduced to in the city of the big churches. Police Devil brings cookies that are sweet, delicious, huge, and have giant chocolate chips, not little ones like Chips Ahoy. You love chocolate and love food. He tells you to work for the cookies. You ask what you have to do. He names it and you do it. Then he gives you the cookies.

You eat the cookies, after throwing up of course, and it hurts to swallow, so sometimes you wait a while before you eat them. Once, Little Sister found your cookies and wanted to know where they came from. She ate them and you were furious because she stole your food. You never steal her food. You always share. This time these cookies that you worked so hard for are gone and she says she knows how you got them and she's gonna tell Honey. You don't want Honey to know about this work you're doing so you shut up.

Little Sister will steal from you a lot through the years and always justify it somehow. Still, you're not ashamed of working for your food. After all, you're hungry, and nobody else is giving you cookies. Besides, this is what whores do, and you're a whore. Everybody says so, so they shouldn't be surprised.

Police Devil showed up one more time with cookies. You are not sure what happened to him, he just never came back. Not because you want to, you think of him often when you eat chocolate chip cookies.

Beloved Mother Leaves Devil – Again

The first time you remember Beloved Mother leaving Devil you're in third grade. It had happened before, you are later told. Beloved Mother made friends at the trailer park. These friends moved to Mississippi where they set up a Christian Summer Camp For Teenagers so they could have a place to have fun but not get in trouble, whatever that means. The camp's next to a fast-flowing, strong and deep river. The whole family went there once on vacation.

In suitably dramatic fashion, Beloved Mother manages to throw four kids into the back seat of a VW Bug, strap a tent to the top though she forgets the stakes and poles, shove clothes and a few other things into the front trunk, and take off while Devil is in town running errands.

She cries and drives and says you kids will never, ever have to worry ever again about that mean man because she is leaving him — leaving and never coming back! — and you finally make it to a gas station out in the middle of nowhere in which state you're not sure but it is open all night. Beloved Mother says she needs to sleep before she can drive any farther. She parks at the side of the station, tells you kids to stay in the car, don't get out no matter what, and leaves the car running so there will be heat.

Little Sister and Baby Brothers have to go to the bathroom and there is one right over there and you haven't seen anybody, so with Beloved Mother dead to the world as she always is when she sleeps, you get everybody out and herd them to the bathroom. When you come out a police car is next to the VW Bug. You herd the kids back to the car, open the passenger door, and all pile in.

The policeman knocks and knocks on Beloved Mother's window but, as he finds out, she's dead to the world and never wakes up. He asks what you're doing here and you explain she is sleeping so she can continue driving later. He says to get back in the car and turn it off or else everyone will die of some sort of poisoning the likes of which you can't remember because you never heard of it.

You tell him you've been in the car for a couple of hours now and nobody is dead, so you think all will be well. The policeman gets the same look on his face Beloved Mother does when she doesn't know what to do with you. He nods, you get in, and lock up. Beloved Mother wakes up a little while later, checks to see you're all in the car, and takes off for Mississippi and the friends who own the Christian Summer Camp For Teenagers, though it is winter and there will be no swimming this time.

You manage to make it to the friends and hear Beloved Mother in another room as she pours out her story and you hear them praying with her. You peek through the not-quite-closed door and see one friend praying hard. You know she is praying hard because she keeps sucking up her spittle that threatens to drip onto her hands holding Mother's hands.

You cannot bear to watch and stop peeking.

However, you've managed to hear the story Beloved Mother tells her friends and wonder where it is she has been living because the story she's telling is nothing like what your lives are like. According to her, Honey and she are having small lovers spats. You want to walk in and correct her, but have a feeling interrupting prayer to God might not be a good thing and walk away.

Before too long, Forgetful Mother and friends come out of the room. They're all smiles and Forgetful Mother says they are right. She must forgive and forget. So she makes a phone call and in a few hours Honey arrives at the airport having flown in to claim his wife and children who left him.

Isn't this a silly little misunderstanding?

Yes, baby, sweetie, I forgive you.

I love you.

I love you, too.

Boo-hoo. Boo-hoo.

Giggle and smile and beam and Beloved Mother twinkles up at Honey.

Christian friends beam at the kiss-kiss-hug-hug, happy airport reunion between Beloved Mother and Atheist They Believe They Might Save. You stand there, disgusted at the show they are putting on. After a two-day vacation with the Christians, all expenses paid by them, of course, during which time everyone is smiling and laughing and nobody gets beat and you don't have to twinkle, you all pile into the VW Bug and head east. Christian friends stand arm in arm waving tearful goodbyes as they bask in the glow of their Christian duty done.

You analyze the situation the whole way back to Georgia. Beloved Mother promises he'll never be a bother again. She breaks her promise because there he is driving, holding her hand, and smiling. She doesn't tell her friends the truth. That you understand because, after all, you know the importance of not talking to strangers about life at home even if the strangers are friends. Still, if she was really leaving and never going back, you cannot understand why she couldn't have told the truth. What could he have done?

What could he have done?

The Toe Burning

Devil loves to have his fun with his cigs. He throws down a burning butt and tells you to put it out. He gives explicit directions as to how to perform the task with style.

Stand next to the burning butt.

Lift leg slightly.

Cock boohiney out to the side.

Lower foot.

Grind slowly with toes only, the grind of course accompanied by a slow swivel of the hips.

Yeah. It's all about style, and since Playboy Bunnies must have style, you practice. As time goes on, of course, Little Sister wants to get into the act and she races you to the butt and stomps it flat. No style at all. Devil rolls his eyes. Then Little Baby Brother, who adores his daddy, starts racing, too. Only he always is barefoot and one day he manages to get to the burning butt first. He, unlike Little Sister, has style.

Stand next to the burning butt. Lift leg slightly. Cock boohiney to the side. Lower foot. Grind slowly with toes only, and slowly swivel hips.

He looks up at his daddy, waiting for approval of his stylish execution. The butt wedges between his toes and now his flesh melts. His smile and happy laugh turn to anguish and screams. Honey jerks him up and scrapes off the burning butt. His foot's burned badly. Honey screams for Beloved Mother and together they rush him to the hospital.

There are three things you most remember from that incident. One: You had never seen Honey upset over any of you getting hurt. Two: Honey never threw down a burning butt again. Three: Honey was kind to Little Baby Brother until he got better.

This goes into your catalog of things to process.

Marty and the Panties

In fourth grade, you meet a little boy whose name is Marty. Marty can jump higher than anybody you've ever known. You tower over him, but his legs are so strong he can jump higher than your long ones ever thought of doing. Each day you're in awe of his ability and he can't wait to show off at recess. You form a mutual admiration society based solely on talent — you never think of kissing Marty and he never mentions kissing to you.

Each day you challenge each other to newer, greater, bigger, higher, faster, and each day he outdoes you. You don't care because this is not a contest to see who can outdo the other, but rather an opportunity to stretch your limits and encourage and be encouraged.

You adore Marty and he adores you. You never talk of anything except physical skills. Still, Marty outdoes you even though you're very athletic and mostly outdo every boy and girl in everything, so this is a new experience. One day Marty asks if you can climb the rope to the very, very top. This you've never tried before and begin the ascent when you hear several girls screeching your name at the top of their lungs and telling you to come down now.

Barely up the rope, you quickly slide down, and run to them to find out what the emergency is. They huddle around and say you cannot climb the rope. You look at the rope and then your arms and say of course you can climb it, you're strong, you won't fall. They shake their heads and tell you again. It is obvious you're missing something.

They whisper dramatically: Your panties will show.

Panties. Will. Show.

You slowly repeat those words until you understand them. It had been two years since you last thought of panties; you knew you wore a pair today and everything was covered so you didn't see what the problem was and say as much to the girls.

One whispers: Good girls don't let their panties show. The others nod agreement as they advise you on this most important panty etiquette.

Oh. Well. That's clear then.

It's okay to let your panties show because you already know you aren't a good girl. You are a whore. You don't tell the girls this, though. You shrug as if they are wasting your time, turn, run to the rope and, with Marty below spotting, climb to the top and skinny on down again. The girls run to the teacher and tell on you. Marty never mentions your panties; instead he tells you how you looked going up and how to get better. You both practice.

Marty was great. You often wonder what happened to Marty because one day he just wasn't there. Or maybe it was you that just wasn't there. More importantly, you wonder if Marty ever remembers you because you've learned something else about yourself:

You want to be remembered.

You want your goodness never to be forgotten.

Beloved Mother, Little Sister, Baby Brothers, and even Devil and Honey never seem to remember anything good about you and the negativity of their lives is too much to bear, more so even than the pain they inflict. You want to be a good girl even though you aren't.

Marty, do you remember the good girl?

[2020 **Author's note:** I tracked down Marty using a Facebook private group I found for the elementary school we attended. I asked if anybody remembered a Marty and sure enough, we got in touch. He had gone into the military then joined the Atlanta police. After retiring, he moved to the country with his wonderful wife. I told him about the book and sent him a copy. He was excited to read it. And guess what? He remembered me! He said he always rode his bicycle by my house hoping for a glimpse of the cute girl. Then, sadly, one day she was gone and he never saw her again.]

Teacher Murders Painting Man

On Main Street, a teacher and his wife and kids lived in the house next door. They rented the bottom floor from Beloved Mother. You're not sure if they lived there before Suited Devil whose windows you tried to cut with the special tool that only made scratches, or after Suited Devil left when the windows got repaired. Doesn't matter anyway. A traveling painting man rented a room upstairs while he was on a job.

Painting Man and Teacher are big buddies and like to get drunk together. But, when Painting Man gets drunk, he doesn't know when to shut up, and he always insults somebody. When Teacher gets drunk, he gets mean, and he hits people when they don't shut up. So, not a good combination. When they weren't drunk, they liked each other fine, so the drinking would always begin with them liking each other fine, then things would turn ugly.

You're in the other house when you hear screaming coming from the house with Teacher and Painting Man. Honey and Mother run next door.

Beloved Mother comes running back to the house, telling you kids to stay inside, do not go anywhere, and with shaking hands calls the police.

If Beloved Mother's calling the police, who are not welcome at the house unless it's Police Devil who's friends with Devil, then you know something very, very bad just happened. Beloved Mother is paler than you've ever seen her, and after the call, she runs back and brings Teacher's wife and kids who are every one screaming and crying.

The police, stationed just down the street, arrive quickly with sirens and lights and all that stuff, and next thing you see is Teacher, handcuffed, put in a car, and taken away. Honey comes back to the house and tells Beloved Mother he can't make the call, she will have to.

Beloved Mother wails and asks why her, some discussion ensues and she — like always — does as she is told. She drives to Painting Man's house where she tells the wife, whose five kids are asleep: You are now a widow.

It seems that Painting Man hollered from the top of the stairs down to Teacher something that Teacher took great exception to. Teacher ran up the stairs and whacked him a good one, but not enough to kill him; Painting Man just lost his balance and fell from the landing, over the balustrade, and down the stairs. Neck broken. Dead right there.

You hear, though you aren't sure, that Teacher killed himself in jail after he got sober and found out what he did. You thought that was fine for Teacher to kill himself, and you wished Devil would feel sorry for what he was always doing and kill himself, too.

Devil never will oblige.

Candy Corn on Main

Little Sister and you spend many happy hours exploring Main Street; you're in the end of third and all of fourth grade during this time. From the hardware store to the sign painter to Marie's Gift Shop, you watch things and people, and learn where to get stuff. One thing you're still always on the lookout for is food Devil cannot control, and that Beloved Mother hasn't cooked.

You don't want to have to beg permission to eat a bite or two, and you certainly don't want to stand in a line with Little Sister and Baby Brothers and Beloved Mother as Devil slowly enjoys his New York strip steak — perfectly prepared by you and only you because, according to Devil, nobody else in this house can do it like you. He talks about each bite as he cuts it, holds it up for all to see as he says he wonders who will get this bite, then slowly puts it in his mouth and chews with what teeth remain.

So hot dogs at church on Wednesday nights? Oh, you're there; you don't have to fake an interest in God either. Or Ronald McDonald making an appearance at the McDonald's down the street? You're there, too, even if you do have to sit on his lap to get the certificate for a free hamburger and fries. Baby Brothers go through the line several times until finally Ronald says hey, haven't you boys been through here before and they lie and say no, at which point Ronald says they better not come through again or else.

Big Baby Brother says you should go through again. You tell him you can't because, unlike he who is not as memorable, Ronald remembers you. He says Ronald would for sure give you as many certificates as you wanted if *you* sat on his lap, and gets mad when you don't go get more food for them. He didn't understand the rules very well.

So you and Little Sister are always exploring and keeping your eyes open for food when, up the street, on the sidewalk for all to see, is a pile of candy corn. You look around hoping no one else has spied it. When you get to it, you pick up all of it, hoping and wishing it will not be claimed before you can make a getaway.

Little Sister, while also wanting the candy corn, is hopping mad you're getting it off the sidewalk. She keeps screaming something about germs. You tell her to shut up, you don't see any germs. In fact, there isn't even any dirt; she should lighten up, for Pete's sake. She refuses to eat it when you offer and — her loss — you shove it in and chew fast before somebody can take it away.

Several men walk by and notice what you're doing. They smile or laugh, so obviously it isn't going to hurt you to eat this free food. Little Sister watches, simultaneously jealous you got the candy and she did not, and impressed you had the guts to eat all those germs.

She was always conflicted like that.

The Chore List

Honey gathers you and Little Sister in the living room one day when you're in fourth grade and explains about this thing called chores. He takes the liberty of drawing up a list and if you do everything on the list for one whole week, you each will get one quarter.

One quarter's big money. In your world that's one giant Baby Ruth candy bar. You both sign on for this gig and lists are issued with the explanation of each day x-ing out the ones you do. It's a complicated system and, furthermore, he'll be checking to make sure the quarter is earned. For every chore missed, even for one day, one nickel will be subtracted.

The first week goes fine and you get the quarter. The next week you're not sure what happened and somehow miss doing some chores. You miss so many that not only do you not get your quarter, Honey's now saying you owe him. You specifically remember that part of the deal not coming up and protest. It's one thing to not get what you never had. It's quite another to lose what is already yours. This is unfair and you say so.

Honey doesn't like your tone. He never spanked or hit you, but your logical reasoning, passionately delivered, made him mad. He said you had two choices of punishment for such insolence. You could either get three licks with The Leather Belt delivered by him or give up riding your bike for one week.

Little Sister tells you to take the beating, but you ignore her because she always wanted to see you get beat. You choose to give up your bike for one week because, while you could handle pain for others, you can't handle your own pain even though you had been practicing for years by digging into your belly button with a needle and making it bleed after getting all the lint out.

So one whole miserably long week goes by while Little Sister taunts you with her bike riding and says I told you to take the beating. You never miss your chores after that and figure out a different way to make your case with Devil because, unlike Beloved Mother and Little Sister, you learn from mistakes.

Mother Finds Religion – Again

Beloved Mother rediscovers religion when you're in fourth grade. Contrary to her usual confessions to you, it's years before you found out what motivated her to make a stand for God this time. Here's the story.

Beloved Mother got sick and tired of getting beat and having her money taken and seeing her children treated badly. So she waits until Honey is gone, runs a tub full of warm water even though it's summer, and is getting ready to call you in and drown you, then your sister and two brothers in turn, when she has an epiphany.

She isn't the problem. The kids aren't the problem. Honey is the problem.

Her next epiphany is just as clear. She'll accidentally kill him. She loads the shotgun and, in defiance of his explicit directions to the contrary, sits in Honey's naugahyde easy chair awaiting his return from whatever fun he's out having, and practices her story.

Oh, officer, it was terrible. He was showing me how to use the gun and it accidentally went off, boo-hoo-hoo.

She knows the police will not believe her, not really, though she feels confident they will let her get away with it because, after all, he is a local drug pusher and is always causing trouble and attracting other lowlifes. They'll help her with the details of the service she's rendering. Besides, she's very pretty and knows how to cry. She feels sure she'll get away with Honey's execution.

She hears a knock at the door. She answers it. There's a man and his son wanting to talk to her about God. She cries, puts up the gun, and her honey, your devil, lives to torment you all another day or two or year or decade. At the time you're proud of Beloved Mother for taking a stand for God against Devil's wishes. Devil's even more miserable toward her about that. It isn't because he cares one way or the other what religion she has. It's just another opportunity to give her a hard time.

So each time Beloved Mother goes to meeting, Devil tells you how much fun you could be having doing something wonderful if only she was here. Something wonderful like going to the beach and having a picnic. You commiserate with him, though you never understand why all of you couldn't get in the car and go and she could join you later.

Still, you, who wanted to learn about God and walked to church wherever you lived, were now forbidden to go with Beloved Mother and she was forbidden to talk to you about God. And she didn't, unless asked something in particular, in which case she'd answer in a whisper and if Honey walked into the room, the conversation stopped, maybe never to resume.

This must change.

Marie's Gift Shop on Main

In front of the A&P Grocery on Main Street is a small block building next to the Feed and Seed. The farm supply store smells of chow for various animals and once a year they sell baby yellow birds of some sort, though you don't know why they can't get them all the time. You love the smell because it reminds you of the barns in Texas where you spent many happy hours licking salt blocks and sneaking sugar cubes out of burlap sacks, some of which you gave to the horses who loved to see you coming.

Anyway, there was Marie's Gift Shop in the white block building and one day you and Little Sister gather the courage to see what a gift shop is all about. A little bell tinkles when you push the door open and step into the coolness. A woman, white hair and obviously old, old, old, sits in a chair.

Hello, she said, who might you be? That question began months and months of visits you, and sometimes Little Sister, enjoyed. Your middle name is Marie, though you never used it, and here was another Marie with a gift shop full of things you saw no practical use for and all of which were easily broken and would never last at your house what with Devil always throwing things and such, but you sure did like talking to her.

As is your routine in any store, you and Little Sister look at everything, see the cost, count your money, and discuss the merits of spending precious funds. Usually the decision is to pass and move on to the next item. This routine is followed even more closely at Marie's, where you never buy anything. Until one day Little Sister excitedly draws attention to a box full of Grab Bags, all affordably priced and some heavy. You do not understand the concept of spending money on something you cannot see.

You want Marie to let you look inside and pick the best. She patiently explains that the whole purpose of the Grab Bag is that it's a surprise. You don't like surprises, explaining further you had to make sure you spent your money where it counted the most. Marie sees the dilemma and says to let her give it some thought and come back another day. You nod as Little Sister shakes each bag, making guesses as to what might be inside.

A few days later, per your agreement with Marie, you and Little Sister open the door, and there she is, happy to see you. You know that because a big old smile lit up her face and she says she's solved the problem of the Grab Bag.

Little Sister wastes no time and immediately begins comparing the weights of each, setting out only those that are heaviest and make some sort of noise when shook. Marie says nothing. Then she turns to you and explains that no matter which bag you choose, she is sure there will be something in it beneficial to you. If you disagree and cannot find any use for it, she will allow you to choose another.

How much does that option cost, you ask. Marie explains that whatever you spend on Grab Bag One will go toward Grab Bag Two. Little Sister is still shaking and comparing and making recommendations. Marie's as good as her word and every few days when you get some extra cash from picking up Coke bottles along the road and turning them in to the A&P for the deposit, you swing by and go through the routine again.

Then one day, sitting in the Grab Bag box is the biggest bag you ever saw. Little Sister and you stare, then she picks it up. Her eyes get big because she can barely lift it. This has to be the one today, get it. The cost is a little more than you normally spend, but it's five times bigger than anything you ever got before. Marie watches patiently as you do the math in your head and reach the conclusion she knew you would.

Little Sister tears open the paper. You are both speechless — for different reasons. There before you is the biggest, prettiest glass jar full of every kind of fancy-wrapped candy ever.

Little Sister blinks and licks her lips.

You immediately start worrying. You tell Marie goodbye, hold the jar close, and walk out. You both know you can't go home until you have a conversation; walking to the back of the A&P, you find a curb, sit, and place the troublesome jar on the ground at your feet and stare at it.

You see, nobody at home knows you and Little Sister buy stuff. Everything bought is small enough to hide from prying eyes as you arrive. This will take days to eat and the jar's too big to hide. You and Little Sister don't want Devil to take it, and he will if he sees it. You also know Beloved Mother will show it to him, too, because she always does stupid stuff like that, so you think and think.

What to do? Little Sister says this is too big of a problem and Beloved Mother really should be consulted. You agree. Little Sister opens the candy jar, you each take out two pieces, eat one, and put the other in your purse. The lid is put on tight, the jar set against the building, and you walk across the street to the house.

It doesn't take Beloved Mother long to make a decision. Go get it, she says, I'll make sure Honey doesn't steal it. So off you two take, running across the street to grab up the giant jar of candy, and — it is gone.

Gone!

Little Sister and you look high and low as you each question the other: Are you sure this is where it was?

Inconceivable it could disappear so quickly. Beloved Mother is not happy. She tells you from now on to bring home those things. Such bounty never happened again until Rockey gave the family a whole cow cut up and frozen.

Anyway, you never tell Marie what happened.

When you're nineteen, and live in Northeast Georgia, you drive to Main Street to visit Marie's Gift Shop. Was she real or just your imagination? There it was. Same white block building. You park in the A&P lot.

Will Marie be there? You stand outside looking at the sign, take a deep breath, turn the handle, hear the tinkle, and there she is. Still sitting in the same spot. She smiles and says hello, it's been a while, my you sure grew up to be a pretty young woman, sit and visit.

And you do.

She asks about your life and your adventures and as you tell the unvarnished truth about your life since you last saw her, you think you see sadness and anger flash in her eyes, but you aren't sure because she smiles the whole time.

Of course now, as an adult, you know what Marie did for you and Little Sister. You know she knew Beloved Mother and Devil and she hated the situation and the kindnesses she showed were all she could do to bring something good to your existence.

The visit with her isn't too long. After all, you have a long drive home, need to sleep at some point and go to work at midnight. And there she is and you feel better knowing she is real. Mostly you want to be remembered because you need to be remembered. You need to matter to someone enough that they would think of you.

Marie remembered you.

Marie did not forget you.

Marie made you real.

Preacher Autographs the Holy Bible

As the family moves around, you and Little Sister always find a church to go to. For some reason they all ended up being Presbyterian. The Episcopalian name scared the bejesus out of you both and you gave those churches a wide berth. The Methodist church reserved pews and the preacher, choir, deacons, ushers, and parishioners all took a mighty big dislike to you sitting in the stacked pews closest to the preacher. The sermon stopped and all eyes fell upon you and Little Sister as an usher walked gravely to the front, up the stairs, and asked you to move. But why?

When you were told these seats didn't belong to you and a long finger pointed to the engraved gold plaque with somebody else's name on it, you asked why you still couldn't sit there seeing as how those people weren't there, and why should perfectly fine, up-close seats be wasted?

The long finger opened the little gate, and the usher the finger belonged to stood righteously ramrod straight. The congregation held its breath as you and Little Sister stood and walked down the steps to the aisle, down the long aisle, and out the front door. And you didn't like their boring Sunday School class, either. To hell with them.

In this other church called Primitive Something, people thumped their Bibles and screamed a lot, flopping here and there. You were out of there in a flash hoping a devil didn't follow.

So you end up at Presbyterian churches. Not that those were any better at teaching you about God. At least they don't ask you to move when you sit up close and they don't scream and they serve hot dogs every Wednesday night. All you can eat. And a Coke that you drink even though you're only allowed one on Saturday, but you drink it anyway because God provided that one and who is the Devil to tell you you can't eat God's food?

By this time you're in fifth grade. You figure you'll spend as much time as possible at the church and maybe, at some point, they'll get around to mentioning something specific about God and His Son. You're not too keen on the fact that God is a daddy because by now you already stopped wishing for your daddy and daddies couldn't exactly be relied upon, but maybe, seeing as how He is God and all, maybe He's an okay daddy and you keep going.

The Presbyterian churches are full of rich people and the other little girls let you know you don't fit in. But why? They say it's because you wear the same old raggedy dress too small for you. You tell them you wear this because it is the only dress you own fit for going to church in and you cannot afford any others. See, they say, rolling their eyes and holding their noses: Exactly, you don't fit in.

You look at them with that stare you've perfected. The one that says I don't give a shit if you live or die so you will remove yourself from my presence now or suffer the consequences. The stare that leaves your eyes flat, cold, dark, no twinkle to be found. The stare that saves you plenty through the years. The girls see the stare and blink. When they blink you know you've won and they will never bother you again, and they don't. So you go about the business of learning about God.

You ask questions of Sunday School Teacher and she is happy to answer. After about four questions she says, you know, maybe she better call in Reverend Preacher, he'll know those answers. You wait for the next Sunday.

The next Sunday there is commotion outside the door of the class. It opens with a flourish and a deacon announces the arrival of Reverend Preacher. You don't like Reverend Preacher because the first time you went to church there you saw everyone lining up at the front door to shake his hand. You stood in line also. You watched as everyone shook his hand; you wanted to learn the protocol and do it right.

It becomes your turn. You nod, hold out your hand and begin to say something nice about the sermon. Reverend Preacher takes your hand and moves you past him and out the door with a quick force and smiles at the rich people in line behind you. You don't like him, but maybe he has answers and Sunday School Teacher seems to think so and you like her, so you wait.

Reverend Preacher approaches, says the answers you want are in this book, shows you the front of it — Holy Bible — then writes something in the front, and hands it to you. He stands there. You nod and say thank you. He sighs, leaves the room, and Sunday School Teacher looks from you to him. This is not what she expected him to do.

You open the book and notice Reverend Preacher put his name in the front of the Holy Bible. Nothing else. Just his name. You look up at Sunday

School Teacher with cold, flat, dark, non-twinkly eyes. You are not happy and she knows it. Fine. You have nothing better to do and nowhere better to do it, so you stay at that church until the family's next inevitable move.

In the meantime, they announce a contest. Whoever can memorize the catechism first, all the way through, accurately, will win five dollars. Oh, that five dollars is yours and you sure could use it. You begin with the first question.

Who is God?

The answer: He is the Father.

You move to the second question.

Who is Jesus?

Well, you already know that, too. He is the Son. This contest will be a piece of cake. You can already feel that five dollars in your wallet.

But you are stopped short because of the answer in the book: He is God the Father.

Huh? This makes no sense at all and you never make it to the third question. So you go straight to the top, bypassing Sunday School Teacher who cannot answer anything. You chase down Reverend Preacher, who is very hard to find, catching him in a hall he didn't know you knew about and is surprised you're in. You say you have a problem with this answer; there must be a mistake here as you point to the catechism.

Within a few minutes Reverend Preacher is furious and you're livid and disgusted. You can't believe what an idiot he is. He can't answer one simple little question to your satisfaction. Reverend Preacher stomps off muttering something that sounds a lot like what Devil says when he's mad at Little Sister. You turn on your heel and stomp off in the opposite direction.

Still, you've nothing better to do and nowhere better to do it, and there are those free hot dogs and Cokes, so you go back to the same church and bring that autographed Holy Bible and you sit and stare at him and he hates you and you wait for him to tell you to look somewhere in the Holy Bible and read something specific and he never does. He waves his floppy Bible around the pulpit and the pages flutter in the breeze of his wave and you watch the parishioners and nobody else in the congregation has their Holy Bible. Maybe his is enough for everyone.

Your ears perk up when he says there will be a special treat next week: A baby will be baptized. You can't wait to get home and tell your still-religious mother — of course, in a whisper when Devil isn't around — this baby will be consecrated and you will get to see it.

Beloved Mother explains the facts, and even cites several passages of scripture, and you have all week to think about it.

The Sprinkling

So you and Little Sister can't get home fast enough and excitedly tell Beloved Mother about the baptism upcoming. Beloved Mother frowns and says baptizing babies is wrong. You ask why. She tells you the Holy Bible says the only ones who ever get baptized are grown-up people and Jesus, God's Son — even Beloved Mother knows he isn't his own father, so how hard can that concept be? — was thirty when he got baptized. She explains that making this decision about God cannot be made by a baby who cannot yet think. It's a personal decision, she says.

This makes perfect sense because you remember how unthinking Little Sister and Baby Brothers were when they were that little and you constantly watched out for them because they didn't know anything. Still, you and Little Sister are not going to miss this event for anything and show up on Sunday, autographed Holy Bible in hand. To get a better view, you sit front row center.

Reverend Preacher calls up the mother, father, godparents, and some other people and they crowd around a fancy bowl. Reverend Preacher intones about this child and about his parents dedicating him to God and a bunch of other stuff you know is wrong because Beloved Mother already explained it to you from your own Holy Bible, but you don't say anything because this isn't your show and that wouldn't be polite.

Reverend Preacher then announces to the congregation that everyone who agrees this little child should be baptized please stand. Little Sister looks at you and you look at Little Sister. You agree you do not agree and remain seated front row center, right under the disapproving nose of Reverend Preacher, who is now looking down at seated you.

All who agree this child should be baptized should stand now, he says again with authority and nods at you both. You and Little Sister remain seated. The parents of the little child have eyes bigger than the bowl they wait beside as they fear the Wrath of God coming down on these two street urchins who are much too close to their precious child. Reverend Preacher says it again. You remain seated. He commands you to stand. You both shake your head no.

He asks if you agree with the child getting baptized. You speak up and say you do not. The congregation gasps as one and hearts are clutched in fear. You are certain women are fainting behind you and men are catching their precious wives' bodies. Reverend Preacher asks why. You tell him Jesus, God's Son by the way, did not get baptized until he was thirty. You tell him all the apostles were all grown up when they got baptized. You tell him about all the sinners who got baptized by Jesus and that they were all grown up. You tell him you read in the Holy Bible *he gave you* where it talks about baptism and couldn't find anything in there that said a baby ever got baptized.

You cannot understand why Reverend Preacher is mad because you were politely and quietly saying nothing; he had to go and ask.

Anyway, Reverend Preacher wants to cuss, and it is all he can do not to throw that bowl of water on you and scream die, Devil Girl, die. The congregation waits and their eyes turn as one to him. He gets himself under control and says that most everybody agrees with this child's baptism and they shall continue. You wait for the child to be dipped.

Whoa. What is this sprinkling thing? The Holy Bible clearly says dipped. You read it in the very Holy Bible that Reverend Preacher autographed. Under and up. It can't be any clearer, and you know about going underwater.

The show ends and you go home and tell the story. You don't bother whispering this one and Devil walks in and you keep right on, not caring if he hears or not. Beloved Mother looks at you, again, like she does not know who you are or what to do with you.

It is Honey who chuckles and says that's my girl.

You like that. Through the years you twinkle as you tell him stories and make him laugh so he'll stay Honey as much as possible. Because when he is laughing with you, he doesn't bother Beloved Mother or anybody else.

Little Sister (left) with Author.

Mr. Hardy

Little Sister and you are always on the lookout for how to make money. When you're in fifth grade, an opportunity arises for cleaning the apartment of one of Beloved Mother's tenants. Easy money, and Mr. Hardy hires you both on the spot and arrangements are made for cleaning his place every other Saturday. The first time you arrive, you and Little Sister dust and sweep and clean his kitchenette.

He thinks you did a fine, fine job, holds out two silver dollars apiece, and says he expects you in two weeks. This arrangement lasts for some time until one Saturday you show up and he says he's so sorry, he forgot you were coming and already cleaned. Your faces fall. You wonder how you'll make the payment on the mini bike you bought on time. However, he continues, he's just beginning a cooking project that sure could use some extra hands and would you mind doing that today for the money instead?

Hey, customer service is what it's all about and cooking was fun, so yeah. And that is how you three ended up spending peaceful Saturday afternoons together making saltwater taffy, baking cookies, or just having a cup of hot tea and yakking up a storm.

Mr. Hardy reminds you of Grandfather, and Grandfather isn't always around, so you and Little Sister love him when Grandfather isn't there. Mr. Hardy came over to the house one day and said goodbye. He's moving on down the road now. You don't know what to say; you don't like goodbyes.

Daddy left you. Horse left you. Snake left you. Now Mr. Hardy's leaving. You nod and he walks away. Little Sister wonders where more money like that can be made. You don't cry over him until years later. Mr. Hardy and Grandfather: The two nicest men in the world because they only wanted to be nice and teach you things and they never, ever asked you to twinkle in that special way, or do anything else in return for being nice and teaching you.

The Ironing Basket

In fifth grade, you live on Harvard Avenue and go to school at S.R. Young Elementary and get the worst teacher of your entire life to that point and forever after. It is here you became frustrated with the never-ending chore that is ironing.

The chore list Honey made for you and Little Sister included ironing five pieces of clothes per day. Five times two times seven may sound like a lot of clothes, but there were six of you and sheets and pillowcases to be ironed, too, so even at five times two times seven, the ironing basket never got empty and was often overflowing.

You became obsessed with seeing the bottom of that damn wicker basket that was almost as tall as you and three times as big around. You would not stop ironing until it was done. Done! Finished! Over! You started the next Saturday morning, early.

During the day Beloved But Tired Mother came in and said she sure did appreciate your doing this. Little Sister came in and said you were stupid. Finding enough coat hangers became a problem. Never had all the clothes been cleaned and ironed and hung up at one time, so some strategizing about where to put things came into play. But finally, there it was: The Damn Bottom.

A piece of paper is at the bottom. The basket must be completely empty. You pick up the paper and under it find a strange coin. You see the date on it — you liked to check the dates on coins — from sometime in the 1800s. But you remember thinking it was strange and take the coin, now late in the evening, to your room and put it in a safe place in a drawer.

At some point the next day, because you want to keep Devil as Honey, you tell the entertaining and grand story of ironing all day only to find this funny coin at the bottom of the basket. Honey's very interested in the coin and asks to see it and you run up to your room and bring it down. He admires it and you put it away.

A couple of weeks later you want to see your penny and check your special place in the drawer where you put important things. The penny is gone. You search the drawer carefully. You scour the room. You ask Beloved Mother if she knows what happened to the penny.

Her slight pause as she began to formulate an answer told all you needed to know. You said oh, he took it. She had the grace to look ashamed and nod. But why? It was only worth one cent; there was nothing smaller than that, and you should know because you made your first long-term transaction over a penny and two Hershey's Kisses. She said the coin was very rare and he sold it for a lot of money. You asked why he didn't come and ask for the penny and share some of the money with you because you found it and it would never, ever had been found if you hadn't slaved all day, outside of the chore list and pay for the week. There was nothing to say, so she didn't reply, and you walked away disgusted.

But Honey felt bad and spent some of the money to keep his promises about teaching you things you'd be very good at. The pool table was delivered not long after and the ping-pong table topper also arrived.

Honey spent hours teaching you how to shoot pool, though you never got as good as he wanted. He couldn't figure out why, though later in life you found out you're nearsighted in one eye and farsighted in the other and you didn't yet wear glasses to help with that.

But with ping-pong, well, somehow you're a whiz and you and he play for hours and practice trick shots and hitting the ball back and forth without looking at it. When his friends come over, the two of you put on shows of prowess and everyone loves you and Honey, and Honey loves you because you make him look good when you twinkle with the paddles.

Still, every time you twinkle with the paddles and attempt to twinkle with the cue, you seethe at the money that could have been put to much better use. Ping-pong and pool: What a waste when food's needed and bill collectors need paying and are hounding Broke Mama.

Honey is Fun

Still, Honey's a lot of fun, and you enjoyed the games and then came the first really nice street motorcycle. The Honda 90 dirt bikes he had when you were in fourth grade were already gone when Honey came home with the fanciest motorcycle ever when you were in fifth. This one had something on the front that would keep most of the bugs and wind off the riders. It had these things wrapped around the front that kept off even more wind. The seats were big and comfortable. The engine was powerful, more powerful than anything you ever felt.

Nothing made Honey happier than late in the evening to holler up the stairs for you to come ride. You'd put on the best helmets that could be bought, of course, and he'd take off with you on the back, your legs holding his hips tight, your arms wrapped around his waist, taking the curves as one.

Often you ended up at the house of Honey's sometime-boss in Kennesaw, a rich man with two families. The first was a legal wife and spoiled daughter (you know this because she had a whole room full of toys) and two sons, one of whom lied about his age so he could go to Vietnam and die three months after he got there and the other who opposed the war and got married on top of Stone Mountain at sunrise, divorcing not long after. The second family lived in the North Georgia mountains and that wife wasn't legal but he had a lot of money and he visited and paid for everything and took care of the kids.

But there you'd be, starting late, leaving Harvard Avenue, running up and down the highways, feeling the power of the engine throughout your body, ending up at Boss' house, and sitting in the living room with Boss and Legal Wife and Honey as if you were Wife and you'd listen to the adult conversation and get tired because you were just a kid and school and chores and homework, stifle a yawn.

That's Honey's cue. He says he has to get you back home and you slowly put on your helmet after saying goodnight and Boss and Legal Wife stand in the driveway and wave as you turn around and wave goodbye to them before you tighten your legs on Honey's hips and lock your arms around his waist and lay your head on his back and sleep all the way home where the next sound you hear is Beloved Mother fussing about getting her home so late and him saying she's fine and stop nagging and can't the girl have some fun as you stumble up the stairs and fall into bed.

So, yeah, Honey is fun. If only Devil would stop showing up so much, life would be great. But Devil gets particularly nasty at this time and you begin a new phase of life. The one where you are big enough to get into the middle of the altercations. But first you must overcome your fear of pain. More practice pain is needed.

Mr. Spock and The Captain's Woman

Attempts to the contrary, you were a child and, like most children, loved to play, though sometimes the games were weird. Star Trek was the best show on television and Little Sister wanted to be Mr. Spock. She was always asking if her ears were getting pointier.

Little Sister made up a great game. She'd make you buy two bags of M&M candies — melts in your mouth, not in your hand. She'd hold up one of the bags and solemnly say that this bag you must not eat fast like you always do. These are energy pills, see, and they must last the whole afternoon as you play Star Trek.

The game is simple. Little Sister is Mr. Spock. Fine with you because, while you liked Mr. Spock, you didn't want to be him at all. But the only other characters on the show you identify with are the captain's women. There's always some woman pining over Captain Kirk and waiting for him. You know how to do that, that's for sure.

With Little Sister's go the game begins. Rip the tops off the energy pill bags. Pop one and only one energy pill into your mouths. Stare at each other as the energy pill slowly melts. Swallow energy pill. Feel the energy pill take effect. Mr. Spock, gravely, reminds The Captain's Woman of the importance of making the energy pills last all afternoon. Mr. Spock speaks into his communicator and lets someone on the ship know the mission has begun. The Captain's Woman is told to take her position and off Mr. Spock goes with a final admonition to conserve the energy pills; after all, the mission will be long.

The Captain's Woman looks around for a place to wait. The cool of the bushes is a fine spot. So there The Captain's Woman sits and waits for Mr. Spock to return and take her to the captain. And she thinks melts in your mouth, not in your hand. Is that true? She determines to find out. She opens her bag and pulls out one energy pill, just one, for experimental purposes only since it isn't time to charge up again. She can report her findings to Mr. Spock and won't he be glad to get that technical information? She puts it in her hand. She closes her fist around it and — dang, it does so melt in your hand.

Crap. Now The Captain's Woman has a problem: A chocolate mess in her hand and it's going to get all over her clothes if she doesn't wash up. But she cannot leave her post. What if Mr. Spock comes back and finds her gone and leaves her behind on the mission? Oh, perish the thought that the captain would have to wait for her.

Lick!

Mr. Spock arrives shortly. He parts the bushes with a scientifically delivered hello, Captain's Woman, how are your energy pills lasting? He screams at The Captain's Woman because she is dumping the last of the energy pills into her mouth.

Disgusted, Mr. Spock lays into The Captain's Woman, telling her she will never survive the mission and get to see the captain if she has not enough self-discipline to make her energy pills last all afternoon. Mr. Spock stalks away but doesn't tell The Captain's Woman where he's going.

Game over.

More Belly Button Lint

Only one other time does Devil make you and Little Sister stomp Christmas tree balls. Devil's ideas about what was fun changed often. Practice with the needle making blood in your belly button came in handy that Christmas and you weren't as scared when you stomped. You managed to make sure Little Sister didn't stomp but one or two as you hogged all the fun while she screamed you were being unfair. She wasn't very smart sometimes. Devil thought you were great as you twinkled madly among the shards of glass around the slowly emptying Christmas tree.

Still, that didn't stop you from practicing blood and pain. After all, there was no telling when Devil would demand something again and you had to be ready. So here you are in fifth grade, still getting rid of belly button lint and getting sick to your stomach from the pain but making the blood flow anyway, going on wonderful motorcycle rides, dealing with a psychotic teacher who chooses you as her personal whipping girl, and listening as night after night you hear Beloved Mother quietly accept her torture and beg him to stop.

One night you decide this must stop and sneak down the stairs avoiding the squeaky spots on each step and hide behind a door and look through the crack.

Beloved Mother has a sewing needle and tries to put a button on a shirt. She is having a hard time sewing because Devil has a cigarette in one hand and her hair in the other as he slowly brings her to her knees as she begs for him to please not burn her. You watch and then walk down the hall to the kitchen, get a cast iron frying pan and come back to your spot behind the door. Clutching the pan to your chest, you vow that if Devil burns Beloved Mother you'll kill him with one blow to the head. This you vow while silently pleading — with God or the Devil, maybe both, you are never specific — to please, please, please not let Mama get burned.

Because the shameful truth is this: You are scared and know you will not be able to save Beloved Mother from this thing called burning. You didn't know that was something used on purpose for pain and what if he hears you coming and grabs the frying pan and burns you?

You have not practiced that pain and won't be able to practice it because he would miss any cigarettes and, besides, it's burning.

Burning. No. No. No. Can't do that.

The fear that leads you to silently plead for your own salvation is something you will be ashamed of for years. Devil doesn't burn Begging Mama and after a while he tires of his game and she goes back to the sofa and finishes sewing on the button while the television stations shut down for the night and the jets from the airport take off one minute after another, making the house shake.

You sneak back into the kitchen, shamefully shaking with fear, and you put the frying pan back and momentarily think you should clunk the pan as you put it down and hope Devil hears, but you chicken out.

Yella-belly!

You hear them getting up and going to their bed and you hide in a closet in the hall and wait until they've gone and sneak back up the stairs and crawl into bed with Little Sister, who sleeps like the dead.

You practice on your belly button so much it stays raw and doesn't heal. That's okay because the shame you feel at your fear is overwhelming. You are a coward. A yella-bellied coward. And as Devil has told you time and again, there is nothing worse than a coward. You must make sure Devil never knows you are a coward.

And you begin to analyze this new information so you can remain The Big Helper that Beloved Mother now needs more than ever.

Confess, or Else!

Devil wants to know who wrote on the wall. There it is, big as life, a drawing in crayon. You don't remember what the drawing was, and it doesn't matter. It was just a little kid drawing on a beautiful open space that was begging to be used as a canvas. All of you understood about canvases; Devil's an artist and there are plenty of them around the house.

You remember seeing Devil's expression when he stood in front of a large white canvas, stretched and nailed to the backs of the strips of hardwood frame. One tiny wrinkle, one small wave, and he'd go off on a well-reasoned but angry harangue against the person who didn't pay attention and put out such sloppy work, so he began building and stretching his own. Do it yourself if you want it done right, he says.

You remember listening to him explain about filling in the blank area as he tells you what the painting will be. You see the passion in his face as he explains about prepping the canvas for the acceptance of all colors. As he squeezes the tubes of oil paint onto the palette, Honey reads their names: Burnt umber, cobalt blue, yellow ochre, vermillion red, titanium white, cadmium yellow, and more. The names thrill you.

Fan brushes and boar bristle brushes in all shapes and sizes, fat pallet knives and skinny ones, too, easels big enough to hold a canvas six feet tall, the smell of turpentine and paints, the canvases and the rags, the mixing of the paints to form other colors: What wasn't to love about this most creative and mysterious of activities any of you ever saw?

Was it any wonder you kids would be inspired to use the biggest canvas of all: The wall.

But, that made Devil mad and he lined you all up from oldest to youngest and demanded one of you confess now, or else. You all knew what *or else* meant, and of the four of you standing in front of Devil, two knew the truth.

You knew who drew on the wall. Little Sister hadn't done it and she stood staring up at Devil wondering when someone would say it was her and getting ready to perform her dodging-the-belt screaming dance. Little Baby Brother didn't do it and he, still young enough to believe that truth will out and justice still existed, stared at Daddy in complete faith it wouldn't be him that got beat. Big Baby Brother, who usually got the worst of the beatings after Beloved Mother, was scared of what was coming and you, watching him without looking at him, saw he was torn.

Should he confess? Yes, but he didn't want to get beat that day.

So it was on this day you managed to believe that maybe, somehow, you could take a beating for him and save Big Baby Brother.

A crucial decision was arrived at within a couple of seconds of Devil's command to confess. You knew you couldn't wait too long to speak because if you delayed Little Sister and Little Baby Brother would think you might be trying to pin something on them. And if you said it was Big Baby Brother, well, he would have felt betrayed and that just wouldn't be right. You step forward, put yourself between Devil and the rest, and confess.

I drew on the wall.

Little Sister breathes a sigh of relief. Little Baby Brother simply watches. Big Baby Brother's eyes go wide; gratitude and relief is written on his face.

Finally, finally, finally, thank you God, you aren't gonna be a yella-belly anymore. You will finally feel the same pain as everyone else and will live through it and be one of them. Finally, your cowardice is faced as you step forward into the line of fire.

I drew on the wall.

You remember those words, not because there was anything special about them, but because this was the day you stepped up, you did right by Big Baby Brother.

I drew on the wall.

The words are said with all the sincerity Devil taught you to use when lying. Shoulders back. Spine straight. Head up. Clear gaze. Speak. Dip the head and lower the eyes. He taught you well.

Devil's gaze is filled with such love. Proud he is of you. Yes, he is, and you bask in that glow, God help you. More importantly, though, you save the kids and you aren't a coward and the beating with The Leather Belt will soon begin. You feel good. You feel proud. What will the leather feel like as it hits your skin? Will you be hit across the back with the buckle like Baby Brothers are? Will you scream, cry, and dance around like Little Sister?

I drew on the wall.

Yella-bellied coward no more. This is a good day. A good day indeed.

Devil's next words horrify all of you. He looks at you and says he knows it wasn't you and that it was one of those little bastards that did it and because they let you confess, it will be all of them who get beat and you, his own little shining twinkler, his precious Little Con, will go free. Devil moves you to the side of the room, away from the arc of his swing.

Little Sister gets it first, and her dodge-the-belt dance is a beauty. She screams it isn't fair. Her beating wasn't too bad because Devil always had a hard time controlling her twisting body. He also knew she was a little bit touched, so he didn't lay it on hard like he did with Baby Brothers and Beloved Mother.

Little Baby Brother is next, uncomprehending; he took his less-thanLittle Sister beating and cried and rubbed his butt and stood off to the side, pure mad pouring out as he looked at his Daddy who betrayed him once again, not liking this at all. The betrayal hurt worse than the belt.

Big Baby Brother is last. He knows the beatings are his fault. He does not fight the beating. As if lashed between upright posts in the middle of a prison yard, readying himself for the cat-o-nine-tails, he stares ahead, avoiding your sickened gaze, stands tall, straight, and when the belt falls and falls and falls across his back and his butt and his arms and his legs, he barely flinches. This is deserved punishment, let Devil pour it on — and Devil does.

Two thoughts come to you. You're still a yella-belly because you're glad you missed the beating. Yet you are mad your pain tolerance went untested.

Big Baby Brother's raw welts and broken skin remind you for days to come: There is no justice in this world and there never will be.

Monkey

Honey comes home with Monkey, a new pet you use to practice showmanship. You put a leash on him and take him for a walk around the new city to which you just moved. You live in the same house Beloved Mother dropped you and Little Sister off at for a year when she wanted to play with her new honey, the Devil. Grandfather kept the house all those years. He said he was moving to the Florida Keys to fish and his daughter and her husband and children needed a place to live, so there you are, starting sixth grade, back at Beloved Mother's childhood home taking Monkey for a walk.

Monkey likes to walk and you make sure you take him plenty. One day, for reasons you have no idea, he becomes violent, biting and clawing your face and pulling your hair with all his might. Even as he is fighting, you manage to get him out of your now-tangled hair and chain him on his perch. You tell Honey, who gives you a length of wood and says the next time he hurts you, use this wood to hurt him in the same spot.

A couple of days later, Monkey begs to go for a walk. The walk is a success and you get home and sit on the front porch, in the shade, side by side. Then out of the blue, Monkey leaps to your head, uses all fours to grab your hair and bites the bridge of your nose. The pain is excruciating.

You grab Monkey by the collar with one hand and pull him off as he shrieks and claws and you calmly hit him with all your might — and that is hard because you're very strong — across the nose. You let his collar go, though you still have the leash. Monkey grabs his nose and howls and flops around on the porch writhing in pain. You stare with eyes flat, dark, but aren't angry. Finally, Monkey is sitting beside you quietly patting his nose and occasionally stealing glances at you. He looks you in the eye and from that moment until the day he too leaves, he never is violent with you again.

In the summer between sixth and seventh grade, Beloved Mother is at work, Grandfather is busy, Honey is gone on a trip, and all the kids are out playing at the school playgrounds. The house is empty all day. Grandfather, back from the Keys, gets home first, opens the door, smells a stench coming from the inside, and immediately closes the door. He doesn't want to clean that up.

Beloved Mother arrives home from her current waitressing job, tired and worn out, pockets heavy with tip change. She screams when she smells it and runs inside opening windows and doors, barely avoiding stepping in the carnage of shit splattering the walls, splotching the furniture, covering the floors.

She hears moaning coming from the kitchen. Monkey is on top of the refrigerator, on his back, his head and arms hanging off. His moans are horrible and he is covered with monkey shit because he is lying in a pile of monkey shit. Mother picks him up gently and carries him to the tub to bathe him. She must clean the tub first.

How did Monkey get out of his cage and how did he come to fill the house with his shit? After Monkey is carefully laid in his cage to rest and the lock refastened, Beloved But Tired Mother begins the process of cleaning and it is in this cleaning the mystery is solved.

See, Monkey loves chocolate more than anything. He can't get enough of Hershey's Milk Chocolate candy bars. So when he breaks loose from his cage, it's only natural he should go searching for chocolate. Which he finds. In the bathroom. In the medicine cabinet. The entire box of Ex-Lax chocolate laxative is empty. Monkey never wanted chocolate again.

Monkey is like a lot of people in your family. He wants what he wants no matter what, and will only change his ways when the pain is too great.

Monkey was sold to a lady who loved cocaine. Monkey got loose in her apartment one day and found her stash and ate the whole thing. Poor Monkey. What you'll always remember, though, is that he was happiest when he could swim in a tub full of cold water. He'd jump in, hold his breath, go under, push off with his feet and shoot from one end to the other until he came up for another breath, sink under, and go again.

You watched him for hours because you understood his happiness and freedom. You knew what it's like to swim with the dolphins, though by now you knew to hold your breath when you went under. You were such a silly little girl to think dreams were real.

Poor Monkey.

Always the New Kid

It isn't like you're the first kid whose parents move a lot and they have to always get used to a new school. Most of those kids had parents in the military. Everybody else tended to stay put, so most of the time you're coming into classes where every kid in the room has been going to school together since day one. You step right into ongoing feuds, changing allegiances, and old grudges looking for revenge, often becoming the pawn as kids attempt to use you as their secret weapon.

Fortunately, you don't play those games and see them coming a mile away. Your responses don't fit within their sphere of experience. So when two girls in fifth grade, who had been best friends since first, chose you as the thing over which they would fight, you became friends with both; neither knew how to play that game. The girl drama was ridiculous.

And as is par for your course, the good boy falls in love with you as does the bad boy, the smart boy, and the jock. Then all the girls are mad at you.

You're also highly competitive. You don't play kickball or any other game to lose. You know how to focus on the play at hand and tune out everything distracting. The boys love it even though you often beat them and they get mad; the girls are scared of the competitiveness.

In Miss Jane Chapman's sixth grade, though, you feel more a part of a group, even though Perry wants to fuck you (so said his sign language and note) and Sammy follows you home every day begging for you to like only him. Even though you kick Sammy in the shins. Even though you hit him on the head with your metal lunchbox with the glass-lined thermos. Even though you call him names. Sammy just will not give up. Still, you're part of something and for the first time get asked to help with an after-school project for the community.

A float needs to be decorated for a parade. Can you help? Sure. Then you're told to get permission from your parents. This is an unknown situation. Never before have you ever asked permission because if you did, you'd never get an answer or the answer would be no and for no good reason. You ask why permission has to be granted and are told a tale about parents needing to know where their kids are and some such stuff as that.

Again, you do not understand. Parents worry about their kids? Huh. Still, you want to work on the float, so you get in line with all the other kids to call home and ask permission. You listen to each kid. Since you never had to call home before, you try to remember the number.

Then it's your turn.

Please let no one be home, you wish. The phone rings and it's answered by Devil masquerading as Honey. You explain the project and that you need his permission to work on it. He makes you explain again. You try to sound like it's no big deal but he can tell you really want this thing. He tells you sure, you can stay on one condition: You have to say, where everybody can hear you, please, Honey, please.

You hold the phone to your ear, planning your response as he repeats himself. Say it, he says. Say please, Honey, please. You want to be part of something. You want to work together with people on this very creative project — a float for a parade! — and he knows it. Say it, he says again.

You feel your heart pound and can't breathe.

Say it, he says again, this time smooth as the honey he wants dripping from your voice, with an added edge of steel.

You manage to choke out: Please, Honey, please may I stay after school and work on this float?

You hear a small laugh of pleasure, permission is granted, and you hang up. When you look up from the phone, the principal stares as do all the other kids. One kid finally says what everyone is thinking: Who's Honey?

You speak in a normal tone, and do so as if this was a normal thing, making up yet another beautiful story to explain away the weirdness of your actions, and you walk away and help with the float. But it sticks in your craw. You vow you will never put yourself in that position again: The position of begging like Mother.

So five years later you're living in yet another town and the family trip is to Six Flags and everybody is in the car and Devil makes you all wait in the hot sun while he decides whether he'll go. He comes out to your car and says he'll drive and you give him the seat. Then he says somebody did something wrong and for that —

You get out of the car and slam the door and get halfway to the front door when you hear where in the hell do you think you're going and you answer: Not playing that game. Go or not, I don't care. Devil says he was only playing, come on, and you get in the back seat and Baby Brothers look at you gratefully because they want to go but Beloved Mother and Little Sister both look at you like who are you and how do you get away with this stuff?

You sleep all the way past Atlanta to Six Flags and have a good day. Everybody else does, too.

Miss Jane, Prayer, and Perry

Miss Jane Chapman is the woman you always wanted to be. She is smart. She is beautiful. She is fair. She can play volleyball and basketball and softball and knows how to square dance and play chess and so many other things you just cannot believe. Boy, can she dress, too; her style is so…so…sexy ladylike. You like and respect her. She is the best teacher you'll ever have, bar none, and sixth grade at Church Street Elementary is better because of her.

The day you really notice her as a person is the day she says it is your turn to say a prayer before the class leaves for lunch. This was back in the day when prayers could be said openly in public school and teachers led the prayers or assigned someone to do so. You thought repetitive prayers were disrespectful, so you were not going to say God is great, God is good, let us thank Thee for our food when it was your turn.

So you say your own prayer, one you make up right there and then, and it's respectful, and you say thank you and ask for help in being good and when you say in Jesus' name, amen, the class intones amen as in church, then looks as one at you and when you raise your head, Miss Jane Chapman looks at you as if to say where did you come from all of a sudden? The class, which normally rushes to the door to get in line for lunch after the God is Great prayer, never moves, and their eyes turn to Miss Jane Chapman as if to say you're our spokesperson, tell her.

And Miss Jane Chapman does. She says she has never heard such a lovely prayer and asks where you learned to pray like that. You don't remember now what it is you answered, but it was something about disrespect of repetition that means nothing; the answer takes her by surprise, and she thinks it's wonderful, and the class sighs and then goes to lunch.

One day, Perry, a boy you like a lot but won't let him know, is making hand signals from across the room. He points to you. He points to himself. Then he slowly pushes the forefinger of one hand through the O of the thumb and forefinger of the other hand, pulls it back out, pushes it back in, pulls it back out, and pushes it back in, while raising his eyebrows. You let him know you do not understand by cocking your head and shaking it a little bit.

He repeats. Point you. Point him. Finger through O. Raise eyebrows. Small smile.

This is repeated several times until he mouths do you want to fuck me and makes the movements again. You are shocked. You give him a look that says no way in hell, Bubba, at which point he says please, baby. You righteously turn your newly Christian head away and refuse to look at him again.

When it's convenient, you tell Miss Jane Chapman what he did and what he mouthed and that you, as a good girl, turned him down. Miss Chapman thanks you and Perry never speaks of it again.

Miss Chapman also knew things you didn't. She always gave Perry the primo jobs in the class. As the bad boy, he should not have been given those privileges. These fun things belonged to people who were good and did as they were told. Yet time after time, Miss Chapman incurred the wrath of the entire class, and one day it came to a head.

Perry had been sent, yet again, to get the cart from the library that held the television. The big television sat at the top and if you didn't push the cart right it would fall off and break and cost the school a lot of money. Perry happily ran out the door of the classroom and when the door closed and Miss Chapman turned to the class, cold eyes turned back on her, accusing her of unfairness.

She never blinked because she knew this was coming. She was so smart. She told the class a story and it went something like this.

Class, I know you think I'm doing something wrong by letting this bad boy do these fun things. There is something I know about him you do not. I will tell you but you must promise me you will never let Perry know you know this about him. Can I trust you to keep this secret about Perry?

As one, the class nods.

Perry is an abused child.

The class gasps.

Nobody loves him, she continues. His family doesn't care if he comes home or not, or lives or dies. He needs someone, anyone, to show they care, to trust him with something, to depend on him. He needs it. So, hate me if you want, I don't care. I'm going to give Perry what he needs even if no one else will.

Then Miss Jane Chapman stared at the class and the class was ashamed. No other words are said and when Perry comes back with the television the rest of that year, the class is happy to see him go get it and says he does such a good job and he feels wonderful even if he does brag about how it's he and only he that gets to do this most wonderful thing.

You feel sorry for Perry because, while bad things happen to you, at least Beloved Mother relies on you to be The Big Helper and she'd miss you if you were gone. And Honey loves you even if Devil loves you more and they'd both miss you if you were gone. And Little Sister and Baby Brothers feel the same even though they are mad at you most of the time. Grandfather loves you and spends time with you even if he does end every conversation with Angie…aaaahhh.

Of course you didn't feel so sorry for Perry that you'd have fucked him if he asked because that is fornication and God says that's wrong. At least you now give him a genuine smile and you understand. And at the end of the year when the school-wide square dances are held, it is Perry who wants to dance with you and it is you who says of course you'll be his partner and you twinkle at him full force and he loves you for it and is a gentleman and thanks you for the dances in a fine and proper fashion. Perry will be okay, thanks to Miss Jane Chapman.

Yes, Miss Jane Chapman is the woman you wanted to be.

Leaving Devil – Again

This time you're leaving for good, Beloved Mother whispers when you're in sixth grade. She promises and again, in suitably dramatic fashion, manages to leave half-cocked and ill-prepared. This has happened so many times that by now everyone knows their parts. Each grabs clothes and climbs into the VW Bus. Beloved Mother drives to Alabama where she checks into a motel across the street from a Kentucky Fried Chicken.

Mother gives you money and explicit directions on what to buy and you and Little Sister walk across the highway and bring back full meals for everyone. The price is ridiculously low for this feast. The chicken is the best you've ever eaten and the biscuit and coleslaw are melt-in-your-mouth delicious. They even give each of you — each of you! — something called a wet nap that smells of cleanliness and you can't wait to wash your hands with the refreshing cloth. Little Sister and Baby Brothers don't use theirs; you squirrel them in your purse.

The next day, Beloved Mother hears there are jobs to be had in a mill nearby and drives over there, then tells all of you to stay in the VW Bus while she goes in. The kids are hungry, it is hot, so you open the doors and they run and play in the breeze on the huge lawn under the trees at the front of the mill.

You bring out some food and a picnic ensues. As you eat you notice Beloved Mother walking out the front door of the mill with a tall, handsome man. He's talking fast.

You can tell Beloved Mother is not happy with what he's saying. She keeps shaking her head no. As they get closer he notices the four children and says think of the children and you sure could make a lot of money doing this thing and it is easy money, you'll be on your back, not working hard and slaving in the mill, you're too pretty for that.

You know what he wants Beloved Mother to do, but she is now practicing being a better Christian and she says children, there is no honorable work to be found here, let's go. The man watches as Beloved Mother and kids climb in the VW Bus and he looks at you and you bore a hole through him with the dead-eye, move-and-you'll-die stare you've perfected. He quickly turns on his heel and walks back inside.

In a couple of days, though, a reunion of sorts happens and you're all back at home in Grandfather's house he is letting you live in.

Just like always.

Nothing will change.

Nothing will ever change ever.

For the first time in your life, you're discouraged and cannot summon strength to even care one way or the other. The discouragement doesn't last long and you smile again thanks to two things.

One: You don't have to leave your sixth grade teacher, Miss Chapman. Two: You read and study the Holy Bible in front of Devil even though he has forbidden you to do it, but he doesn't know how to stop it and this little rebellion feels good.

Torture is Nothing New

Torture is nothing new. You know this because you're reading the Holy Bible and learn lots of people have been tortured. Some during war. Some because a mean person hated them. And some because they did what God wanted even though the Devil — you've learned this one is also called Satan — wanted them to stop obeying God.

The difference between the first and second types of torture and the third is that nobody has a choice about the first two. The third kind is different. People choose to do what God wants even though they know they will be tortured. There must be more about God you need to learn that makes people willing to be tortured for obeying Him.

So, you read the Holy Bible and study it in front of Devil and wait for him to torture you like he has been torturing Beloved Mother since she became a Christian. He doesn't and you're happy because, truthfully, you do not like pain and have stopped making blood in your belly button because you think you've practiced enough already.

You've found a new Presbyterian church to go to and it has a huge playground and Baby Brothers play the whole time while you and Little Sister go to Sunday School and learn nothing. This Presbyterian church, on Church Street, is different than the one on Main Street. The people are friendly. They don't mind Baby Brothers playing and not coming in. They suggest you go get them and bring them in for doughnuts and Kool-Aid between Sunday School and The Big Service, and they come in because food is food and all y'all sure could use some.

They tell you to take the extra doughnuts, too, and help you pack them up. You take them and you and Little Sister and Baby Brothers eat all of them before you get home because you know food you bring home may or may not get to be eaten by the family, so you learn never to bring any home, and every Sunday the extra doughnuts are eagerly waited for by Baby Brothers and Little Sister, and also by you, to your deep shame.

One day, though, you have to give up the doughnuts; you're glad to do so. Devil has called you in and demanded you choose between Beloved Mother's church and the Presbyterian church. Whatever you choose this day is where you must go the rest of your life, says he with doom in his voice.

Choose now, once and for all.

You choose Beloved Mother's church because it is there she is learning stuff you like and you're reading her books and studying this stuff. Even though the people and the doughnuts at the new Presbyterian church are great, you're still hungry, but it is your spiritual core that now must be fed.

Devil is shocked. He asks you to rethink your decision. It remains the same. He calls in Little Sister and Big Baby Brother and they all choose Beloved Mother's church. Little Baby Brother chooses the doughnuts and Devil looks at Beloved Mother with triumph. That triumph doesn't last too long because after a couple of weeks of having to take Little Baby Brother to church and then pick him up, two relaxing Sundays ruined, Little Baby Brother is forced against his will to go with Beloved Mother and he screams and cries.

Then your torture begins in school as classmates notice you changing and demand to know why and when you tell them they get mad and make life miserable even though you've learned it's your job as a Christian to figure out a way to explain to them and you do and then that torture ends and you feel victorious and thank God for this newfound purpose in life.

Of course, more torture comes later because of your Christian stand and it will be by the hand of Devil, but you now feel there is a reason for the torture and since God is involved, you figure He will be able to help out — somehow.

A Difference of Opinion, or Stating Your Case

Anyway, Miss Jane Chapman gives the class an assignment. Choose a topic, research it, put together footnotes, and write a paper. This grade counts the most toward the end-of-year grade in some subject you don't remember now. You pay very close attention to the project, get the details, and do a bang-up job. You know you'll get an A-plus, something you rarely get. It takes weeks to prepare, and finally the day comes to get the grade.

In bold red slashes across the top of the first page is a big fat D-minus.

You cannot believe it and look through to see what you did wrong. Page after page, there is nothing but a lot of words underlined in red. No explanation.

You approach Miss Jane Chapman, the fairest teacher in the school, the woman you want to be when you grow up, and ask for an explanation as to why this perfect paper got a D-minus when it was clearly worth an A.

She explains that one of the prime factors that went into her decision was that you used words you did not understand, so it is very clear to her that you copied the report from already-published sources and did not write it in your own words.

Plagiarize? You?

You are furious, and challenge her assertion. You tell her you wrote, and by wrote you mean crafted, every single sentence yourself and copied nothing — nothing! Go on, you say handing her the paper, ask me what any word means. Go on, you scream quietly as the class goes about their business.

Miss Chapman has never seen you like this and stops dead. She flips at random to a word and calls it out. You give the definition and use it correctly in a sentence you make up right there on the spot, thank you very much. She calls out more and more words and you accurately define and make a sentence with each and every one.

She stares at the paper. You stare at her defiantly. She apologizes and says that, clearly, she is wrong, and you say you betcha, and she gives you the A it deserves. You make sure she records the A in the grade book, take the paper and walk to the desk where you sit, victorious and furious, shaking from emotional overload. This is the first time you remember standing up for yourself and you won't forget it ever.

You were able to stand up for yourself because Miss Chapman stood up for Perry against the whole class and you know — you know! — of all the people in the world, Miss Jane Chapman understands and will listen. You aren't wrong and you hate leaving her at the end of the year. You will be moving again soon and well, other than Grandfather, nothing good's permanent in your life, is it?

God is permanent?

Huh. You'll have to think on that a bit.

Binding the Free-Swinging Girls

You begin seventh grade at Church Street Elementary, but are only there one month before moving. You are happy to be out of that class. The teacher could not compare to Miss Chapman and two of the kids are weird and she won't do anything about them.

It's only the second time a girl in your class has been taller. After years of hearing about how tall you are and being singled out for it, when someone else is taller, you are happy.

Well. Sort of. Admit it, you know you're a little bit jealous because you like the attention and there was this other girl getting it all.

Not only that, the best-looking boy in class is obsessed with her and she with him. They carve each other's names into their arms with razor blades during class and you can't take your eyes off them as they carve.

There has to be pain, but they don't seem to feel it and you wonder at their bravery in making so much blood and it isn't their belly buttons and it isn't a sewing needle.

You hate this girl taller than you for getting the attention, and hate yourself for being a jealous coward who can't make blood like her. So you're very, very happy to leave that class and move to another school and not be reminded every day about your shortcomings.

Then your period starts while you're in seventh grade. You wondered if it would ever come. You're already thirteen and have been hearing Beloved Mother brag for years and years about her period starting when she was nine and she just didn't understand why you weren't a woman yet. You hate her when she says that. But one day there it is. You remember it clearly because she had to tell you how to catch the blood. You didn't know there would be blood. You didn't know what a period was. She had never explained, and if anybody else ever did you tuned it out; then you went to the bathroom and there was blood.

You couldn't figure out what was so great about this mess and needed to know how to stop it. You walk into the kitchen and say Mother, I am a woman today. She stops washing dishes, turns to you, and — you swear there were tears — hugs you. For this you get a hug? You do not understand her.

She knew what you needed and showed you how to use these bulky things between your legs attached to giant elastic. A year and a half later you research a better way of handling this situation and inform Mother, who says only bad girls use tampons. You decide she is an idiot, buy the tampons, and after using them for months, tell her. She is furious and says only non-virgins can use them and you tell her the paper in the box says anybody can use them and you're sick of the mess and you aren't going to do what she wants.

She stomps her foot and commands you to cease immediately. Cocky, you shake your head no, and pretty much say whatcha gonna do 'bout it?

Anyway, one other interesting thing happened when your period started: Out popped these things on your chest whose name you refused to say. You could not even say it about chicken parts, preferring drumsticks and wings only, so you sure as heck weren't going to say it about your own body.

B— Br— It's impossible. Anyway, there you are in this new school. Taller than anybody, yay...sort of. Getting more blood than you ever bargained for and there are these boys in your class, tee-heeing and pointing, and whispering something to girls who give you dirty looks.

For God's sake, now what?

You don't know. This goes on for months; the whole time your b---, br---, boo---, you know, them things on the front of the chest, keep getting bigger and bigger and flopping around. You try to keep your arms crossed, though sometimes you can't hide them or keep them from flopping.

At the same time, Devil is still not letting the family take baths except once a week, so your hair is oily. You feel horrible. He also can't stop talking about your br---, boo--, you know, them things. He talks about how pretty they are, flopping around in their natural state, unencumbered, hanging as God intended in all their glory. Now the Atheist Devil gets religion? He loves your …you know, and says you'll never be like all the other women who aren't free and natural. It makes you sick to listen.

One day, the whole thing comes to a head at school. Tee-hee. Whisperwhisper. Lusty glances from boys. Dirty glances from girls. Two girls, representing the crowd, march over and demand to know why it is you don't wear a bra and wash your hair.

Flat out you tell them.

They're horror-stricken and immediately lose their combative jealousy. One of them asks why Devil does that. There's no answer and you shrug and stand mute, wishing to die, wishing for them to walk away, wishing to disappear, wishing for a bra and shampoo. You watch the two girls walk back to the lusty boys and the jealous girls. Whisper-whisper. The boys look at you, no longer lusty, their decent manhood offended. The girls simply cry.

You become invisible where you stand and go away in your mind.

When you get home that afternoon, you storm into the house and demand — demand! — to be taken to the store and a bra and shampoo bought for you. Beloved Mother says it is impossible because Honey won't allow you to have a bra and shampoo. He walks in and you continue demanding.

In front of Devil you tell her you don't care what he wants and that day, before you go to bed, you will have several bras and you will have shampoo and, furthermore, you will take a bath whenever you want to. Honey just smiles and nods to Beloved Mother and you and she go to the store. The next day you wear your stretch-as-you-grow bra to school and your hair is clean. And no one ever, ever brings that subject up again.

You've often wished you could thank the girls and boys in that class for feeling horrified for you. Their speaking up and questioning spurred you to stand up where you might not have done so.

The Excommunication

Devil's next game is pretending to become Sainted Christian. How better to know the enemy than to study them? He learns about a very interesting thing used to punish. It is called excommunication and he decides this is what will be done — to you.

Your period has just started and your b---, br---, you know, those things growing on your chest are still flopping around and you don't have a bra yet and you must take a bath only when he says you can and that is about once a week and somehow or another he is studying the Holy Bible with the family and he doesn't like something you did the other day and it gets brought up and he just about makes a federal case out of it.

The short story: You are bad and must learn your lesson. You will be excommunicated from the family. No one is allowed to talk to you. No one is allowed to look at you. The official excommunication ceremony happens during the family Holy Bible study.

Be banished, young evil girl. Go. Leave the room. We shall look upon you no more until you confess your willful sin and learn your lesson — oh, that again. Devil sure does like to put on a show and the family is impressed. They had never seen an excommunication before, and that it is to be done to the eldest sister they all hate to love and love to hate, well...showtime.

You stand, lay down your Holy Bible, leave the room, and iron in the dark. It is too much to take but you might as well use the time to empty that damn basket again.

You hear your name called. Sainted Christian Devil says you must be present, but are not allowed to participate. Listen, you young rebellious hellion you...destined for eternal...unless you learn your lesson...and listen well for you shall...hear the very words I speak...need to repent, you flagrant sinner.

Blah, blah, blah, blah...you tune out the rambling and sit and think about God and justice and idiot parents and your life and you never repent and never confess and never learn the lessons he thinks he's teaching. And the thrill of excommunicating someone from the family wears off and it is never done again and nobody ever brings it up.

As usual.

Clutch

Clutch showed up one day at the Red Oak house. An obvious mongrel, but aren't they always the smartest dogs? Baby Brothers name him Clutch after a cartoon character popular at the time; it fits him because Clutch is their adventure hero. Another dog lives with you, too. A papered, yappy, snippy weenie dog with a bad attitude. You hate him, but he sure loves Mother.

So when you're moving to North Georgia for Mother to manage a motel, it makes sense that only one dog can come along, and Clutch, who needs space to roam and live outdoors, can't live at the motel, so Yappy comes and Clutch has to remain in Red Oak where he'll have more space than in the little town to which you will move and live in the middle of.

But what to do about Clutch when the move happens? It makes sense to pack up, drive away, and not put him in the car. He can't keep up for long and he'd find another home. But, no; in suitably dramatic fashion, the family has to make a production of it. Beloved Mother loads up kids and Clutch into the VW Bus.

Clutch isn't stupid. He's never been asked to go anywhere with you before; he knows what's getting ready to happen and has to be coerced into the vehicle. He gets in, but he's not happy about it. Resigned to his fate, he sits in the floor, tail tucked, staring ahead, eyes dead. Beloved Mother drives until she finds a farm where a farmer is out in the field. At that time in Atlanta, that wasn't so far.

She drives down the dirt road until she's halfway to the house. The farmer in the field stops what he's doing and stares. You watch to see if he'll say something. He doesn't but you can tell from his face he knows you're getting ready to dump yet another damn dog on his farm and he's mad about having to kill another stray.

Beloved Mother stops the Bus. By this time she's bawling, as are Little Sister and Baby Brothers. Baby Brothers clutch Clutch while saying goodbye, goodbye, goodbye, and getting him wet with their tears. They love Clutch; they had such wonderful adventures with him in the woods. He was simply the best dog ever.

You have to be honest and admit you shed tears, too. Sure you did.

Beloved Mother tells you to open the sliding door on the side. She says to push Clutch out. Clutch doesn't want to go and drags his butt and digs in as best he can with his toenails. You are crying hard by this time, yet do the job. Clutch accepts his fate and his front paws slowly drop to the ground while his butt stays in, then you gently nudge his little butt and he slithers it to the ground with a dejected thump.

You try to catch his eye, but he refuses to look at you, staring instead into his bleak future, one where other betrayals will come and others abandon him no matter how good and helpful he is.

You tell Beloved Mother to tell the farmer he is a good, good dog and will be helpful on the farm, but she can't breathe and can barely drive for the tears in her eyes. She shakes her head and takes off, leaving Clutch in a cloud of dust and Baby Brothers in the back seat, staring out the back window, crying and screaming for their dear — and only — friend, and screaming names at you because it was you who pushed him out.

By the time you get home, everybody is dried up, and faces are resigned, hearts more numb than you ever thought they could be. It's one thing to treat people badly, but it's just plain wrong to desert a defenseless animal.

The Return

Seeing as how Devil is always one step ahead of the law, there's never been a reason to return once a place has been left. In fact, you did not know people went back anywhere after they left.

By the time this first return visit happens for you, the family has moved to where Beloved Mother has been asked by Boss, whose second family lives nearby, to manage a small motel in a small town in Northeast Georgia, onehundred hard miles from Atlanta. One day, Honey, who has pretended to change from Atheist Devil to Christian Saint, says you're coming with him and visiting friends at Trailer Park.

Your first thought: Trailer Park is still there? It ceased to exist when you left and you had not thought of it since the end of second grade. Second thought: What friends?

You get on the newest fancy motorcycle with Honey after putting on the best helmet money can buy and take off for the south side of Atlanta. While holding your legs tight against Honey's hips and keeping your arms wrapped tight around his waist, you think about this new experience.

Visiting a place you used to live. It's still there. Does that mean the other places you lived still exist? It must. What will happen when you get there? Will it look the same as you remember it? How will you act? What will you say? Will you know the people? Will they remember you?

So you show up at the house of the boy who told on you and Jimmy Joe Johnson for playing show-me-yours in the woods that day. Everything from that time rushes in on you and you wonder if he remembers what happened in the woods and wonder if he'll ask you about it. What if Jimmy Joe shows up? Will he still be mad at you for confessing when you were forced to? What if his daddy comes along? Will he want you to dance? Well, you don't dance anymore, so you will decline, but what if Honey wants you to and makes a fuss about it? What then?

The stress of thinking about it wears you out and you stop thinking. So you show up and the boy and the girl and the parents are happy — happy! — to see you. Why, they remember when you weren't nothing but a little girl barely this tall and look how tall you are now and just as pretty, yes, just as pretty, don't you think so, they say to the high school boy who isn't as old as you thought and is looking at you with a smile.

You have not spoken a word because you are mute. The boy asks if you'd like something to drink and at your nod he goes into the kitchen and brings out a tall, clear glass with tea in it. Only everybody is laughing as he hands it to you and you don't know why.

The boy asks if that is enough tea. You look at the glass and see there is only about an inch of tea in this huge glass. You nod seriously that it is fine and drink it. The laughter stops and the boy, whose joke isn't anymore, smiles and says he'll get you a full glass now. When he comes back and hands you the glass this time, he does so with an expression of concern and raises his eyebrows and you manage to croak a thank you — for a croak it is because you are mute. Crossing your legs, like a lady should, and sipping your tea with pinky extended, this is the most twinkle you can manage on this day.

You remember nothing else about the visit, and can never say whether or not Jimmy Joe or his daddy showed up, and the next thing you know you're back at the motel that is still there even though your universe has been ripped open and it is late at night and you fall into bed.

People remember you? Well, how about that.

Hot Pants? Maybe. But no Jiggling.

Hot pants come into fashion in your early teens and, of course, Honey wants you to have some of them short shorts. Your boobs pop out more, you take a stand against Mother and totally go to tampons, men and boys whistle at you everywhere you go, and you hate it.

You do not want to be pretty and do not want to shake anything. So you practice walking as if you have a steel rod for a spine. No hips will swing and your arms will cross over those boobs and they will not bounce. No sir. No way. No how. You would not draw attention to yourself. But nothing helped.

Now the challenge is to see who can get you to turn around and make a dirty face when they honk or whistle. You refuse to play. It doesn't take much to stir up fun in a small town.

So there you are, forced to wear these stupid hot pants, walking like a robot, and working at the motel behind the counter checking people in and out. Often you're there alone with the family out and about doing things. White collar, blue collar, it didn't matter; when they saw you behind the counter they assumed you could be had.

Hey, baby, why don't you come to my room?

You'd say you were only fourteen or fifteen and some said that didn't matter. Others it shut up after they said you sure looked older.

One group of commercial painters stayed in Unit 12; it had two double beds and room for a rental cot so it could sleep five. You check them in and woohoo girl, ain't you just the hottest thing? Betcher wild, ain'tcha? Five men, tiny office, you're alone. You stare them down and they laugh, then leave after you take their money and give them the room keys.

The switchboard phone rings a little while later. It's Unit 12.

Hey, we don't have any soap in this room and we sure could use some because we need to take a bath. Can you bring some down to us, honey?

You know for certain there is soap since it was you yourself who cleaned the room earlier, and tell them so. Maybe they should just look a little harder and you hang up.

Ring.

Hey, we don't have enough soap seeing as how we're so dirty and all.

Okay. Fine. They were awfully dirty. You go into the storeroom, get out several small bars of soap and, coming around the back way so they can't see you immediately, sneak up to the door, knock and run to the middle of the parking lot, ready to flee.

The door opens. A man sees you standing way on out there and laughs. The rest of the men crowd around and laugh, too.

You want soap?

Yeah, baby, bring it here. Woo, girl.

And like the big league pitcher Grandfather wanted you to be, you remember your pitching training and chunk each one of those bars across the parking lot and into the room. The men jump back when the first bar hits one of them, and before the last soap makes it to their door, you're running back to the office and locking the doors with their laughter following you up the hill.

Still, you almost failed to spot a real devil-man one day. You're outside knocking a tennis ball back and forth with Little Sister when a customer walks up and begins to compliment your fine racket form.

You never had a man compliment your skill and you like that. Well, there was Marty that time, but he was a boy. You smile at the man. He knows a place where there are private tennis courts and he would be more than happy to take you and — with a nod toward her — Little Sister, of course, and give private lessons seeing as how he used to be a professional player. Little Sister says she doesn't want to take tennis lessons and the man says he'd be more than happy to give you solo lessons.

You discuss the situation with him and think this is a fine idea. You're tempted to do what you always do: Whatever you want without asking. You almost go with him. But, something niggles at you and the niggling gets insistent. You try to ignore it but can't.

Then out of your mouth pop words you never said before and never say again: Sure, let me go ask Mama if I can go.

The man blinked, and that's when you knew you made the right call. Your gut told you this was a devil-man, a new kind: The helpful sort who offers knowledge and learning. You go to Mama and inform her she should step outside and say you cannot go because you have chores. Now-Useful Mother steps onto the porch and tells the man you're needed for chores. The man politely nods and says of course, I understand, maybe another time; he knows there will never be another time and smiles sadly.

Mother watches him walk to his room. Then she looks at you like what was that all about and goes inside.

Devil is Mad and Doesn't Speak to You

It begins in eighth grade and ends one year later in ninth. Devil walks by. He whispers. Cunt. Whore. Bitch. Fucking liar. And other inspired combinations of those, and other cuss words and insults, and keeps on walking. He stops addressing you directly. Though you're in the same room, if he wants you to do something, he tells Beloved Mother to tell you; she dutifully repeats it. If there's a question you ask him, but he does not look at you and turns his head to his wife, who then repeats the question.

You wait for this new turn of events to end but it goes on for months. After a particularly long and drawn-out three-way conversation one afternoon, when Devil leaves the room, you turn to Beloved Mother and finally ask what is going on. Why is he so mad?

She heaves a frustrated sigh, closes her eyes, tilts her head up and to the side, and pauses. She opens her eyes, unhappy to see you still there. Look, she says as if this is all your fault, Honey is mad because he wants to have sex with you and knows you will never do it again.

She turns on her heel and stomps off. She doesn't see you smile.

It works! Believing in God and taking a stand for Him is keeping Devil away. You laugh and you laugh, and every time Devil whispers cunt, whore, bitch, fucking liar, or any other version of insult, you smile at him because you're smiling the smile that God has given you — tortured finally for taking a stand, not just on general principles.

Not getting the result he needs and wants, Devil decides to change tactics. You come home from school and, in suitably dramatic fashion, you see Devil has hung a long leather belt in front of the door to your bedroom. It is a belt all the kids in school will love and try to find for themselves and you're the first to have it. Hanging on its end is a note: I'm sorry, please forgive me.

You forgive him because isn't that what Christians do and you're doing your best to be a Christian. You never say cuss words. When you walk down the street you never swing your hips because you will not be a whore, no not you, never again, and whores swing their hips. You talk to everyone you meet about God and His Truth and His Future Plans and His Righteousness and you're sincere about it.

Not that you love God, even though the Holy Bible says you must. You can't love Him because you cannot feel love. You respect Him. And you appreciate that He took the time to write this book that has been, finally, some help in figuring out this world and your place in it. Your place is not to be a whore, but to be the one through whom wonderful information will flow.

You learn to twinkle for God and do a damn fine job of it, too. Everybody says so. Many years later you learn you can't twinkle on cue because to do so makes you a hypocrite, and you tell God you can't twinkle in the same way for Him anymore but that you know He understands because, after all, hasn't He been watching since you were a little Big Helper?

Mr. and Mrs. Mickey Mouse Check In

You happen to look out the window at the motel and see one of the boys you go to school with going into Unit 5. A yellow VW Bug is parked in front of the room and a woman gets out carrying a full brown bag and follows the boy in. It seems odd that anyone would rent a room in the town in which they live because that's just a silly waste of money. So you ask Beloved Mother why she rented a room to your schoolmate.

She said she had not done so. So you tell her what you saw and both of you go to the office and pull the registration card for Unit 5. Imagine her surprise when she sees Mickey Mouse and wife, Minnie Mouse, had checked in. They listed their home address as Donald Duck Lane in Disneyland, California.

Mother! Don't you read these things when people check in? No, she does not. Mother walks to Unit 5, knocks on the door, and tells the lady she's with a boy in the ninth grade. The lady whips her head around and screams you're in ninth grade?

He failed a couple of grades and heavy facial hair indicated early onset of prodigious testosterone levels; still he's jailbait and now she knows it, kicking his butt out, and apologizing to Mother. The next day in school he asks why your mama had to go and ruin his good time. You have nothing to say because you don't understand what's so good about that. He says he's gonna take his business to Star Motel. You allow that might be a very good idea, indeed.

Big Helper Gets Her Marching Orders

While it is true that Little Sister, and eventually Baby Brothers as they came along, look to you for help with Devil and getting food and such as that, they also hate you. You'd think the four of you would have pulled together, been a team, loved each other, and had each others' backs seeing as how you had a mutual enemy, right? That state of affairs did not exist. Here's why and it wasn't anybody's doing except Devil's and Beloved Mother's, though it took years to understand her role.

After Beloved Mother brought you back to Devil, they still wanted to party and somehow, though there was a lot of money for pleasure, there never was enough for a babysitter except for that one time when Babysitter lived with you in Texas and Florida, and he wasn't nice.

Anyway, Beloved Mother would get all dressed up and say she'd be back in a little while and don't go outside and look after Little Sister so she doesn't get hurt. Devil added that if Little Sister is bad and won't do what you say, you must beat her with The Leather Belt. When Baby Brothers came along, the instructions were the same.

They'd walk out the door and be gone, sometimes for twenty-four hours, sometimes for two days. There you'd be, four years old and in charge of the house and Little Sister, fifteen months younger. Little Sister, born mad, as soon as they were gone usually tried to do something to hurt herself. You'd have to fight her to keep her from doing it. She wouldn't like that and she'd get madder and madder until she was so out of control you didn't know what to do.

Then you'd remember The Leather Belt and beat Little Sister with it after begging her not to make you do that because you didn't like to hurt her. She'd keep on and keep on, forcing you to beat her. Beloved Mother said to keep her safe and Devil said to beat her and so you do, having tried everything else. Then Little Sister gets calm, you find her some food, and she goes to sleep.

As you get older, Devil adds to your list. Make sure, he'd say, they get their chores done. If I come home and these chores are not done and you haven't beat them to make them do them, you get beat, understand?

You do. You threaten to beat, and occasionally do beat each and every one of them, gently though, never leaving a mark. There comes a time when threats of a beating don't work and they torture you because they can and won't do their chores and they all say they hope you get beat.

You don't want to get beat. It was pain. You hate pain. You must avoid pain at all costs. How to make that happen? Easy. When threats and gentle beatings don't work, you simply solve the problem by doing their chores. Big Baby Brother always laughs contemptuously. Little Sister sneers and calls you names. Little Baby Brother never says anything; he just watches and waits.

This goes on for years, ending with a showdown with Mother when you're fifteen. When you live at the motel, you're often left alone to check in guests while the family does things. You get up and clean rooms before school. You cook. You do the grocery shopping. You clean the house and do laundry. To get these things done you often tell Little Sister and Baby Brothers to get their chores done.

One day they complain to Beloved Mother who then comes into the living room with the three of them — two righteously indignant and one watching — trailing behind her. Beloved Mother demands to know why you think you're the mother of the house and acting in that capacity.

You answer that somebody has to do it. (You could be quite cocky.) She gets mad and wants to know why you started doing it in the first place. You look at her, not believing she said that. You say as much. She asks for an explanation, which is then provided:

Don't you remember from the time I was four, you and Devil putting me in charge and telling me I have to whip them and make sure they get their chores done or else I would be in trouble? You really don't remember telling me that for years, and still telling me, by the way, except no longer does The Leather Belt get mentioned?

She said she did not remember and furthermore you were to cease and desist from being mother from this point forward.

You sigh and say thank you in a smart-alecky way and tell your siblings they are on their own now. They smile and like it, though later when they didn't have you to remind them of their chores and got in trouble when they didn't do them…well, two of them got mad about that, too.

Still, The Big Helper, her duties diminished, was not unneeded.

Drunk Postmaster and the Chicken Dinner

Your first official job, special uniform needed, is at the Tastee Freez across the street from the motel. You are fifteen and Honey hangs out there a lot. He gets you the job. Rockey owns the place, and he and Honey are big buddies.

You need the money, and so are motivated to quickly learn how to take apart and put together the ice cream machine, clean and stock, even cook. But Rockey says you're pretty and he wants you up front to greet the customers.

After a couple of months you and another pretty and well-liked girl are keeping the place rocking and it becomes very popular with the boys from the Technical Institute just out of town. They come in and flirt and you treat them just like you treat everybody else: Take the order, call the number, hand out the trays. Nobody ever gets the courage up to ask you for a date, not that you even try to interest them in it. You're on the job and nothing will take your mind away from it.

One evening the postmaster in town, a cousin of Rockey's you're told, comes to eat with his wife and two kids. Postmaster is drunk as he stands in front of you to order. You ask how you may help. He says he wants a goddamned chicken dinner. Okay, three or four pieces? Goddammit, just give me a chicken dinner. Okay, you write this down.

Wait! Nah. I'll have uuhhh…the shrimp dinner. Yeah.

Okay, eight or twelve pieces?

Just give me a goddamned…no, wait. I'll have chicken.

Okay. Three or four pieces?

His wife is embarrassed and the kids wish they weren't there. You know this because they look just like Beloved Mother and you kids when Devil is pulling something stupid in public.

Four pieces, Postmaster decides loudly; he steps aside so his wife and kids can order. That process goes quickly.

When it comes time to call out their order number, you feel somehow this will turn into a big problem, so you walk the trays over to their table and set the food down in front of each.

Postmaster screams at you. What's this shit? I ordered shrimp not goddamned chicken.

By this time you were in a mood, one that did not want to put up with any shit from anybody and you say, brooking no argument, no sir, in fact you ordered chicken, then shrimp, then changed your mind back to chicken.

The restaurant's packed and everybody stops to watch this show. Postmaster says he did not order chicken and you repeat that he did, in point of fact, change his mind back to chicken.

He says he wants shrimp. You say there will be an extra charge seeing as how he got exactly what he ordered. His family watches closely. Postmaster says he ain't gonna eat the damn chicken and what do you have to say about that, huh? His chin juts out. You say it's his meal and he can do as he wishes with it. He says he isn't gonna touch it and orders it taken away.

And what, sir, do you want me to do with it?

Throw it away, goddammit!

Yes, sir. Of course, sir.

You pick up his tray with his four-piece, perfectly prepared chicken dinner — after all, he is the owner's cousin — and walk to the trash can, hold the chute open, and chunk it in with a flourish of true showmanship. You stack the tray with a bang and go back to work.

Only then does the place buzz again. You watch Postmaster as he sits, hungry, watching his family eat, knowing full well he had been bested but not knowing how. But every time he comes in afterward, he's sober and a perfect gentleman.

Long-standing problem solved — at least while you were there.

The Bad Story

When you're in ninth grade, the home economics teacher hates you because you're a different kind of Christian than her. You really don't care what she thinks because you're going to do what you're going to do and she can just shush. Things get so bad in her class that somehow Mother finds out and has a private talk with her, after which she calms down. You're still not sure how that happened, unless it was one part of your brain that didn't like it and complained repeatedly to Mother — or maybe you were bragging about being tortured for being a Christian. You don't remember.

Anyway, shortly after that showdown, out of the blue comes a writing assignment in Home Ec. Everyone is to write the history of their life. Now there was one thing you knew and that was how to write fiction and reports on other people's lives and history and these were always well written and received.

How can you write the truth and have this teacher not use it against you, Mother, Little Sister, and Baby Brothers? What will happen when she confronts Devil? You — who hated misusing the written word, who reveled in the glory of a well-told story — yes, you must now write truth about your own horrible life.

You give it much thought. The day arrives to turn it in. It's one page. The teacher looks at you and says this is not acceptable. You must tell your entire life history. You take the paper back and rewrite it and it's horrible. All you can write is a series of funny, unrelated incidents while leaving out the gory details. Two pages later, you give it back.

She sighs and takes it. The next day she hands out the graded papers. All the girls are twittering about the wonderful grades and comments and blah, blah, blah. She holds yours to last and says in front of the whole class that she's disappointed in you especially. You, the one who can write. You, the one who can tell a story. You, the eloquent debater of truth. Yes, you wrote a pile of crap and got an F-minus.

On the one hand, a bad grade for writing was the worst thing you could have gotten. On the other, the bad grade guarded the family secrets.

And you knew the importance of that, didn't you?

The Rubber Machine Money

In small towns everybody knows everybody's business, including who's doing who, or at least who's doing somebody because condoms are sold by the bucketful. But you didn't know that.

So while you're working at Tastee Freez during this particular day, a man comes in and asks for a big cup. He goes into the men's bathroom. After a few minutes of clanking and ripping noises, he comes out with the cup full of change, saying to give this to Rockey. You ask what it is and he says it is the rubber machine money.

Rubber machine money?

Yeah, just tell him, he'll know, says the man.

Okay. You, though, who thinks Rockey might not be in before you leave, want to pass on this vital piece of information and take a black magic marker and write in big bold letters on the cup:

RUBBER MACHINE MONEY

You set the cup on the counter where every customer comes to pick up their food. A couple of hours later somebody comes running out from the kitchen in the back, grabs the cup up, pours the change into another cup, destroys the perfectly labeled cup, then turns to you and screams quietly: What the hell is wrong with you?

You don't understand and say as much.

It takes some time before the situation is finally explained: Nobody in town knows about the rubber machine in the men's bathroom and they don't want anybody to know. It's a secret. You say, well, if nobody knows then why does the machine get full of money every few days?

The person looks at you like you're crazy, yet the question is legitimate and you wait for an answer. Finally, unable to come up with an answer, he says from now on you are not to label the cup Rubber Machine Money. Just put the cup back over…here, yeah, here; Rockey will know, he says.

See the Baby?

You're fifteen and Devil has just started talking to you again after a yearlong campaign of silence punctuated with cursed insults. A few months before this event, somebody who liked Honey — or was being blackmailed — pays for the entire family to take a trip to some beach in North Carolina. Mother giggles the whole way up and the whole time she's there. She's even happier upon arriving home than you've ever seen her.

So there you are, in algebra class, and your name is called over the intercom by an urgent voice saying you're to pack up your books and come to the office immediately. You stand, you pack, you walk. Are you moving again?

Arriving at the office, everybody is in a frenzy and worried for you. The principal himself says he'll drive you home. What is going on? No one says in the office. So on the way home from school with Principal, he gently explains Mother lost the baby and you're needed at home to take care of her and the motel while she recuperates. Can he do anything? If you need him, just let him know.

Mother was pregnant? You didn't know, but you don't tell Principal that. By this time he pulls into the parking lot, you thank him, say you will call if he's needed, and go inside.

Honey is holding something. It is a towel or other piece of cloth. He's crying and pacing and wailing and asking God why, why, why? You wonder why the Atheist is asking God, then you remember he's still in his Christian Pretend mode and ignore the histrionics. He stands before you a broken, broken man.

See, he says, as he holds out the cloth and unwraps the most hideous thing you've ever seen in your life. The baby is dead. Well, if that was a baby, then it needed to be dead.

He continues to wail why, why, why? You tell him, gently, to wrap it back up and throw it away, because the children don't need to see this and he should get himself together, the children don't need to see him in this state, either.

You go in to check on Mother while he figures out how to dispose of the grossly formed body, and you end up putting it in the trash can. You run the motel for the next week and look after Mother while she recuperates and then go back to school. Everyone is concerned and wants to know how your dear, precious mother and stepfather are doing in their time of grief. You say they are well and all is well and thank you for the time off and you'll get right on your past-due homework, yes, indeed you will. You get back to the business of being a student, uncomfortable with strangers intruding into your private life.

Mother will have several more miscarriages in the next couple of years and all you can do is wonder why she is still having sex with the Devil.

Twinkling-Good Customer Service

Rockey likes to drink. He's a very, very nice man and helps out your family with food in later years, but he does like the women and he does like the drink and he does like the drama of fighting.

So there he is with this new wife or girlfriend and they're drunk in the parking lot of Tastee Freez and throwing drinks at each other and screaming and fighting and the customers are not happy.

Nobody at the restaurant dares say anything to Rockey because, after all, he could fire them. You don't worry about being fired and aren't scared of the scene in the parking lot. You just know potential customers are driving by without stopping and those who remain are not pleased and you need a job.

You know a business-killer when you see one.

You walk out into the parking lot. Of course, you tell fellow employees inside the restaurant this is what you're going to do and they say you better not or else. Warnings of dire consequences come fast and you ignore them all.

So you walk out into the parking lot. It is night. You holler hey! That gets their attention and they stop and look. Rockey, you need to stop doing that here because the money is drying up. Nobody wants to see your drama.

He understands the money thing in a flash and they leave to continue their foreplay somewhere else. When you walk back in, everybody has the same look that Beloved Mother has: Who are you and where did you come from?

You are used to that and pay no mind. You get back to twinkling for what you now call your customers and they are happy with the service. It makes you proud that you're doing a fine job. Rockey lets you know he appreciates the fine job you're doing and doesn't hold the fussing at him and his woman against you. Even though you never see him again after your teens, years later you will cry when the news comes. He was burned to death in an auto accident on a country side road, watched by a crowd of people who frantically tried to save him but couldn't get him out of the trap before the flames threatened them, too. Rockey understood you and people who understand you are always in short supply.

Still, that is the kind of attention you want: Thank you for a job well done; makes you happy every time. You nod and accept his attention so desperately craved, and work harder. If only Beloved Mother would take a cue from Rockey and say thank you. She never does, you know. At least with customers and an occasional boss, your twinkle is appreciated and you learn well and learn fast to get something positive in life from that.

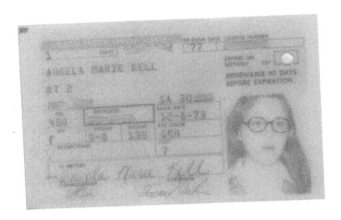

The Driver's License Test

Tenth grade and the talk of the school is always who got their driver's license, who failed the written, who failed the road. The written test is scary, but it never changes and everybody knows what to expect. The road test is frightening because there are only two examiners and one absolutely delighted in failing everybody on their first try. If you got this guy, you'd fail no matter what you did.

You study and the day comes to go to the State Patrol station down the mountain. The written test is barely passed; you never test well, but pass you do. Who will the examiner be?

You get him. The meanest examiner in the whole state. You resign yourself to leaving without a license, though determined it will not be you who gives him a real reason for the failure. You walk to the Oldsmobile. As you open the driver's side door, you hear a hard thump. He's bent over double, holding his knee, walking around in circles, cussing beautifully; you run over to see if you can be of assistance.

Are you okay? What happened? Can I help you? You're following him as he waves you away and says he's fine; even though he can barely talk, the cussing is proficient. He tells you to drive.

You say you can't until he buckles up. Still rubbing his knee he whacked pretty hard on the back bumper, he says he doesn't need to —

He sees you staring, waiting on his compliance. Aaaahhh…he shakes his head, drags the belt around and latches. Drive, he says. And you do — perfectly. You make it back, park, and follow him inside to await the announcement of your assured failure.

Your name is called. Your picture is taken. Someone hands you a piece of paper and says keep up with this because until the other one with the picture shows up, this will serve as your driver's license.

You passed?

You passed! You drive home, a fully licensed driver.

The next day at school, several kids who knew you were going for your license want to know who you got for the examiner. Of course by now you already understood the idea of telling a story for maximum impact. You say, very gravely, that you got Failing Officer.

Everybody says that's too bad and good luck next time. You bat your eyes and say why, whatever do you mean? One boy catches on real fast and he jumps up from the table and hollers you got passed by Failing Officer? Everybody wants to know how that happened, and you tell the story.

They are impressed and the story goes around school about you being the only one ever passed on the first try by Failing Officer. Kids you didn't know threw out congratulations as you walked down the hall.

This wasn't the only time you were congratulated by kids you didn't know. The other time you had no idea what they were talking about.

Oh, by the way, the reason you got to keep a copy of your driver's license when you went for the renewal was because Jimmy Carter, governor of the State of Georgia when you took the test, became president of the entire United States.

The Math Test

ANNOUNCEMENT: All students will take a standardized math test and results will be used for a study…of some sort, you never did understand. But with all the other students, you march off to the auditorium and sit with two sharpened Number 2 pencils and await the packet.

Holy cow. There's stuff on here you've never seen before. You're sure to fail, but bend your head to the test and begin to read; a test, by the way, you never remember putting pencil to, much less finishing.

A few days later you, who never missed school no matter how sick you were, cannot get out of bed. When you come back two days later, everyone is congratulating you again. All students. All teachers. Crowds part as you walk down the hall. Hurrahs blast.

You finally ask what's going on. They point to the bulletin board. You read, not comprehending, when you hear a female teacher say she needs to talk to you about college courses at some places called MIT and Something Tech and you don't understand that either. You aced the test. Made the highest grade in the entire school. How could that be? You make C's in algebra. How is it you outperformed in calculus? What's calculus? You can't afford college. Devil won't let you go to college. Besides, big secret, you're getting ready to quit school because Beloved Mother needs you to work to save money so she can leave Devil for good.

You smile as teachers hug the new star that is you and other teachers plan your brilliant, brilliant future in research and aca-what? You don't want to kill their dreams, so you let them keep them as long as possible. Within six weeks, though, you're sitting in front of a counselor, lying about why you're quitting, and she's begging you to please tell her the truth, please, she can help.

Devil's powerful and it takes special planning to control him. She will never understand and you keep lying. The lie you tell her is not the truth: You are one of God's chosen who will work hard and be a missionary and help save the world. You hate bringing God into this, but He understands. God knows it's never wrong to lie to save someone weaker from a bully. And you're getting ready to pull off the biggest rescue of your life and total secrecy is key.

Wolf

You're sixteen and have not yet quit school. You hear Beloved Mother late at night in the bathroom trying to get ready for work. You also hear Devil. Beloved Mother pleads Honey, let me go, you're hurting me, stop, I'll be late for work. Devil just gets worse, as you knew he would, and ignores her pleas. Finally, you've had enough, get out of bed, and descend the stairs.

You open the bathroom door and step in. Beloved Mother sees you, waves a hand for you to go, and says everything is okay, go, go back to bed. Devil has her by the hair smashing her head into the wall and bent over the back of the toilet and she has her hands against his chest holding on to his shirt pulling him close so he can't throw her too far and pull her hair out.

Devil takes the glowing Camel unfiltered out of his mouth and with it points for you to get out and then says if you know what's best for you, you'll leave. He turns back to Beloved Mother and pounds her head against the wall again and she pleads. You don't budge. You hear yourself, in a voice never heard before, tell Devil to let your mother go.

They both stop and look at you. Devil is thinking he's going to slap you silly and Beloved Mother is believing it, too. You're not sure why, but their eyes get big and Devil's cigarette droops as his mouth hangs open, and she loosens her grip on his shirt. You repeat in that...that voice.

Let. Her. Go.

Devil tries to recoup and swaggers a bit as he stumbles around the words who the fuck do you think you are to tell him? You don't know what he sees; he is now more scared when he looks you in the eye and his hand drops from her hair and he helps her stand up straight. In one last desperate attempt to gain control, he squeaks you gotta leave.

You move not a muscle. You tell him he will leave and allow your mother to get ready for work. He slides past, out of the bathroom, never turning his back.

Turning to Beloved Mother, who is frozen in place and also a little bit scared, you tell her to get ready for work or she will be late.

Years later, after Devil is really dead, Beloved Mother tells you that story. She says she never had seen your face like that or heard that voice. She can't describe it except to say she is glad it happened because you, The Big Helper, saved her that night.

It is some years later, when the doors in your mind are opening and you see all and hear all and remember all, that you know who it was that walked into that bathroom that night. It wasn't Big Helper. It was Wolf. But that wasn't the first time Wolf made an appearance.

The first time was in second grade on the bus going to school. There's a loud commotion at the back. Little Sister, again acting like Beloved Mother and saying something that brings bad attention, is being heckled and shoved by high school students. The more they heckle and shove the more she opens that mouth of hers and makes them want to do it more. You wait for a minute to see if it will stop, though you know it won't. Little Sister screams and hits the floor, thud. She gets up and screams and is shoved and hits the floor again. The older students love this little game.

You get up from a seat near the front of the bus, walk to the back, pick Little Sister up, tell her to get into her seat. The high school students say look, she's being saved by another midget and they make a grab for you. You push Little Sister up the aisle, she stumbles away from danger, and when you turn back to the bullies they gasp, fall back, and get silent.

You remember clearly what was said: Leave my little sister alone.

And you remember how you stood. Legs apart, firmly planted, fists in balls, shoulders squared for the fight. A little midget, for sure, compared to them. There is something about your eyes, though, and your voice, and as one the older students stop smiling and laughing and grabbing. Your eyes are the only thing that move as you look at each of them. Only when satisfied they are no longer a threat do you walk back up the aisle to your seat. Little Sister is never bothered again even when she acts stupid and it is four years before Wolf must make another appearance.

The second time, you're twelve and you and Baby Brothers are at the park playing in the woods, exploring deeper and deeper until finally Baby Brothers find a log over a creek they like and stay while you explore further.

A man pops up in front of you and smiles. You know immediately he is a devil-man and must be controlled. He says hello and aren't you a pretty little thing? You don't twinkle because you know if you twinkle for this devil-man he will hurt you. You say coldly you are pretty and so what? He says he bets you haven't been kissed. You say you have been. He says prove it and advances toward you. You say you don't have to prove a damn thing and he better stop right there or else.

His face changes. He is scared. You have him where you want him. He tries to swagger his way out of his fear and says he bets you've never been kissed by a man. You say you've kissed plenty of men, most of whom are better than him. You stare him down. He says you're all alone in these woods and what's to stop me from kissing you?

You tell him two things will stop him. One: You aren't alone and your two brothers are just over there playing on a log and they will help you kill him. Two: You will be the one who delivers the fatal blow and if he thinks you can't do it just try because he has no idea how strong you are and if he advances one more step, you will call Baby Brothers and if they have to come, it is sure he'll die painfully because they won't take kindly to Big Sister being attacked.

You are Wolf again. You will eat his beating heart. You will tear him limb from limb. The man isn't smiling anymore. He backs away. You stand still, never moving a muscle, and watch with cold, dark, unblinking eyes as he disappears into the woods. Only then do you return to Baby Brothers and tell them it is time to go home.

The fourth time Wolf makes an appearance, you're twenty and getting robbed at the convenience store where you work. Devil-Man Robber holds you privately hostage in plain sight while you check out customer after customer during the rush for holiday beer. He has already shown you the pistol and said he will kill people if you utter a word.

You know how to keep your mouth shut. Hostage situations are nothing new. You manage the bad guy to keep the customers safe until finally no more customers come in. The bad guy says to put the money in his sack of groceries. You comply. Then he pulls out a roll of silver tape and points the gun, telling you to get into the storage room.

This you refuse and firmly say no.

Don't you understand I have a gun, he threatens. You will not go. He spends two minutes threatening and trying to persuade you to do his bidding. It is best to do as he says, the implied *or else* left to hang.

Then he gets scared. The inner voice comes out and says if he's gonna kill you because you know that is what he is going to do after he rapes you, he's gonna do it right here in front of the world because you are not going to cooperate. You calmly command him:

Pick up your sack now.

Take your goddamned money.

And hit the road.

Devil-Man Robber swaggers a bit trying to gain control over the situation, puts the gun in his waistband as another customer walks in, says pointedly this is your lucky day, picks up his sack and backs out through the door, watching you the entire time. You stand still and follow him with your eyes until you no longer see him. You check out the next customers and lock the door behind them. Your manager, who popped in during the event and to whom you managed to mouth we're being robbed when you turned around for a pack of cigarettes, called the police, though you didn't know it and dialed 0 for Operator and told them to please send the police.

One month later you get robbed at gunpoint again; this time twinkle works and he takes the money and peels out of the parking lot, almost hitting a police car, and getting caught. At his trial you feel sorry for his wife and children, who look just like Beloved Mother and you and Little Sister and Baby Brothers did for years and years.

Then a few days after the second robbery, the door opens and in walks Devil-Man Robber. You ignore his existence. He picks up a few groceries. Stands in line. You ring him up. Give him the total. Sack the groceries. And when you go to take his money, he holds it for a moment at which point you look him in the eye and say you know who he is. He has a combination of expressions.

The first is the one Devil has when he calls you his Little Con. It is full of admiration and love and wonder at the creature before him. The second is the one Beloved Mother has when she can't figure you out.

The bad guy can't speak. You give him his change, push his sack toward him, and tell him to move on. He manages a shaky laugh, bows his head briefly, then backs out the door. You never see him or his very icy-blue eyes ever again. That crime is never solved.

Rabbit, Dog, and Turtle Two

On your way to worship one evening, you're alone in the car. Headlights pick up a rabbit running across the road. Thump! You immediately turn around and, shaking and crying, find the rabbit, tear off your winter coat, wrap him in it, and drive him home — hysterical with thoughts of killing Turtle.

You screech into the driveway, hold the coat close, and run in the house barely able to speak from sobbing. Honey jumps up from his chair as you hold out the coat, blubbering and making no sense. Honey knows you and understands there's a hurt animal in the coat and he takes it to the kitchen. When he opens the coat, Rabbit jumps out, off the counter, onto the floor, and immediately hides behind the stove.

It takes some doing to finally get Rabbit back into possession, by which time Honey calms you down by saying Rabbit's okay because look how fast he moves. Rabbit's rewrapped and you drive back to the spot on the road you hit him, and gently place him on the other side.

You put your coat back on and it's full of fleas and they bite, but you proceed to worship, fleas and all.

The next incident happened up the street from the house. A neighbor's bitch gave birth to a passel of long-legged hunting dogs, not full-blooded but close enough, and boy did they like to chase things. One of those things was cars and yours was coming down the street.

Six dogs take off after the car and you slow down trying to miss them. There's always one stupid one in the bunch and, sure enough, that one just had to get in front, get caught under a tire and, being a big dog, roll under the car, thump, thump, thump, thump, howling the whole time. You stop and get out. There's this poor dog, stuck. You have a meltdown. Thoughts of Turtle's murder and your hand in it come rushing in again.

Crying and screaming, you jump back in the car and back up. Thump, thump, thump. Scream, scream, scream. You put it in forward. Thump, thump, thump. You need help; your house is right there so you jump out of the car and run up the street, screaming and crying.

Honey! Honey! Help! Honey! Help.

You had never screamed for his help before and Honey rushes out of the house and you fall into his arms and point wildly up the street. He holds you and walks you back to the car, by which time the neighbors are outside blithely surveying their idiot dog writhing under the transmission case.

Honey gets in and moves the car forward until the dog comes loose. Thump, thump, thump; you keep screaming and crying. The neighbors say well, he's dead. Honey agrees. You won't give up.

No, you scream, we must, we must, we must, boo-hoo-hoo, get him some help. He isn't dead, you insist over and over. Honey and the neighbors stare as you bend double with fear, loathing, and hope that there is something…anything…boo-hoo.

You stand straight. The vet, you scream. Put the dog in the truck and take him to the vet, you'll pay for his treatment. You'll pay!

Honey has never seen you this wild and insistent; he drives your car to the house, gets the truck, puts the dog in the back and you in the passenger seat, and takes off to the vet. You sit in the truck bawling; you can't stop.

When the vet comes you jump out of the truck screaming save him, save him, and cry some more. The two men look from you to the dead dog and the vet says honey, he can't be saved, he's probably already dead.

You will not believe him. How do you know, you scream. You aren't God. He's in pain. Put him out of pain.

He's dead.

No, he's not! Put him out of pain.

The vet said he could do that, and comes back with a syringe full of what he says is a painkiller, and a stethoscope. He listens to the dog's heart, nods, empties the syringe into the dog, and listens again for a minute.

He slowly takes the stethoscope out of his ears and says you don't have to worry anymore because Dog is dead and he died without pain. Only then do you stop being so frantic and simply cry. Honey drives home, patting your shoulder, comforting as best he can.

The third event happens two years later. You and a friend are riding along a back road and crest a hill. You try to miss the giant turtle crossing the road, but it's too late. Your tire catches it. You stop the car in the middle of the lane and look back and see it's still alive but grievously wounded.

You cry. Your friend asks what's wrong. You point back. She looks and, in a matter-of-fact voice, says oh. You remember Turtle from second grade and cannot leave this one to die slowly. You turn the car around and tell your friend you're going to finish the job because it's wrong to hurt an animal and not help it out of its pain.

Tears blur your eyesight; you line up a front wheel with the turtle and will yourself to push the gas. It takes some time to find the courage; finally you floor it and, engine roaring as loud as your screams, you hit Turtle Two and smash it flat. You pull off the road and cry, heartbroken, for ages. Your friend cries too, only because she's worried about you.

Finally, you have to get her home. You suck it up and deliver her.

Some years later, on a steep, straight hill, you see a man in front of you line his tire up to kill a perfectly fine turtle. The anger you show at that wanton murder is nothing like your kids, then four and seven, have ever seen in you or anyone else. It doesn't scare them because you are their trusted mommy, mama, and mom, and they know if you get mad like that, there's a perfectly good reason.

You think back and for the first time marvel that, somehow, in some way, you managed not to become Honey — or Not-So-Beloved Mother — because your kids aren't afraid of you and they trust you for the right reasons.

That made you think about Not-So-Beloved Mother and Little Sister in a way you had not much thought about them before.

Little Sister is Warned

You remember the day as clearly as if you're watching it right now in front of you. Little Sister, sixteen, again works up to taking out her frustrations on you. Today will be the last time she'll try it because you've had enough. She starts with that finger. Poking you in the shoulder and calling you names and daring you to go on, do something about it, you little weak piece of shit who can't stand up to her superior strength.

This day you say it: Stop. She pokes harder. You warn her again. She pokes again but you catch her hand mid-poke and she tries to pull away. You let her go and warn her again: Don't. She pushes her glasses up her nose because they are always slipping and tries to slap you in the face. You stop the blow. This is not acceptable to her. She will beat you again and you will be powerless against her, she screams as the full assault begins. Kicking and punching and slapping; Little Sister is a wild woman.

As usual, she underestimates you. You easily block each blow. She gets madder. She was only playing before, she says, and cuts loose. This time you're forced to hit her. Thud, her body hits the floor. Familiar sound.

Her eyes get big. She screams Mother! She runs out of the room, crying and screaming Big Sister hit me. Beloved Mother comes marching into the room with Little Sister closely following. Beloved Mother sniffs righteously and demands to know why you attacked your poor, defenseless, and weak sister.

You aren't gonna take that either and tell Stupid Mother she is very well aware Little Sister has been beating you for years because she's watched it and you aren't going to let her do it again and you warned her several times to walk away but she wouldn't and you defended yourself. Stupid Mother begins to tell you she will spank you for — You stop her and say she better not touch you because if she does…

Your eyes go flat, dark, cold, no twinkle, and you let her fill in the rest of the sentence in her mind. Mother backs off. Little Sister is not happy. She wants to see you beat and she wants to see you beat good. She tries to force Mother to beat you. Mother doesn't want to because, while Mother may be stupid, she still knows you're the only one who saves her from Honey and she pretty much needs you.

So she tells Little Sister she isn't going to beat you and Little Sister pitches a fit, shocking even Beloved Mother. Beloved Mother tells Little Sister to stop. Little Sister jumps on the sofa and bounces up and down violently, then leaps and grabs Mother around the neck and chokes her.

You pull Little Sister off Beloved Mother, who is standing there unable to move she is so shocked. Little Sister is screaming and crying and now tries to beat you and you slap her in the face because that is what she needs and she finally shudders and calms down, walking into her bedroom like nothing to see here folks, move along.

Beloved Mother breathes hard, holding her hurting throat. She is confused about this turn of events, doesn't look at you, and definitely doesn't thank The Big Helper for saving her once again. You walk into your room, the one you share with Little Sister, who smiles when you get there as if the violence had not just happened, and goes back to reading a book.

You can't wait to go to work in the cotton mill that night and leave this insanity behind. You lie down for a little bit, hoping to have an uninterrupted nap before leaving for the midnight-to-eight shift where you will change out empty cones with full ones of cotton rope in the spinning machines and help the doffers take off the full spindles and refill with empty ones.

The mindless repetition of cleaning chokes, replacing empty cones, dodging the vacuum tubes hanging from the ceiling as they move up and down the aisles like hungry anteaters, shutting down the machine when the spindles are full, helping the doffers doff — all these things are comforting. You can count on them to happen. There is a routine. People say thank you when you help! You can relax at work.

Until the big boss falls in love with you and you tell him Beloved Mother said he was a dirty old man and to leave you alone. Big Boss laughs, though from then on when he comes by your job station he shakes hands professionally and inquires after your health and never again flirts. He later gets fired after being found on the office sofa *en flagrante* with a secretary working hard for the money.

When you tell Beloved Mother about Big Boss being informed he is a dirty old man, she is horrified. She says you should have kept your mouth shut. But — you begin, then stop and think to yourself what's the point? Beloved Mother shakes her head and again gives you the look that says she doesn't know what to do with you.

Damned if you do. Damned if you don't. You can't win and by now you don't even try.

Sheesh. Girls.

Big Baby Brother wakes you. He's covered in mud and says he needs your help and you better come now or else he's going to be killed by Daddy, as he calls the man who always denies fatherhood of him. You drag on clothes, get into the pickup truck, straight shift, and drive deep into the woods across the highway as Big Baby Brother points the way.

There comes a point he tells you to stop and listen carefully. He would prefer to do this operation. You tell him you might get away with hurting the truck but it's a sure bet he never will. He agrees and says okay, fine, you can drive. But listen: There is a small cliff up ahead that must be cleared to get to where the broken-down motorcycle is. That means — do you hear me Big Sister? — you're going to have to go very fast and shoot over it. Can you do that?

You begin shaking. This is a huge deal. What if you break the truck? He assures you that the ground is soft and nothing can hurt this truck if you will just do as he says because he has this all figured out. And besides, you can get away with it and he can't but he'll be happy to drive. You say no and manage to get control of yourself and you put it in first, then second, and you fly through the woods and then, at the last second, lose your nerve and slow down just as he screams goose it!

You don't clear the little cliff and there you are, front tires on the ground and the tailgate stuck good and plenty into the — yeah, he was right — very soft soil, rear tires hanging uselessly.

A young man runs through the woods and he's cussing and saying I told you so and Big Baby Brother is cussing and you're sitting in the driver's seat crying like a girl.

A girl! Oh, shut up, says Big Baby Brother, but you can't and they keep cussing as they dig furiously because time is of the essence and you say you can't help dig because your shoes will get dirty and it's your only pair for work and you can't afford any more and boo-hoo, boo-hoo-hoo-hoo, wah-wah, and so forth in suitably dramatic girl fashion, driving them insane and distracting them from the life-saving work at hand. You can't help it and even though you're furious at yourself for crying and not being the one who can handle this, you can't stop crying and shaking.

Big Baby Brother's friend asks if you're on the rag and you don't know what that means and then you feel the truck drop and they get in the back and tell you where to go and you manage to get everybody home before Devil returns, but it's no thanks to you, and Big Baby Brother can't keep saying it enough times, though no one but you two knows why: Sheesh. Girls.

The Meltdown

The analyzing you began in fifth grade of the new facts of torture has a huge payoff almost immediately. You begin preemptive strikes, though you don't know this is what they are called.

Therefore, if Devil walks in the house a particular way, you know he'll do this. If he sits in his chair this way, he'll do that. You see these patterns, learn them, and often minimize his tirades, the kids' beatings, and Beloved Mother's tortures with advance planning of control techniques.

So one day, when you're seventeen, and been quit school for over a year and working full time from midnight to eight six days a week and as much overtime as you can get, you wake during the day to screaming coming from outside the house. Darn, you weren't there for this preemptive strike and knowing Stupid Mother, she did something to make it worse.

But this day, the entire thing strikes you as beyond your ability to manage in your usual methodical manner. You need sleep. After all, aren't you the only one working and hadn't Devil made you buy a car, putting you in hock to the bank? Don't they know you need sleep, so why are they outside making all this ruckus?

That's it. You've had it. Everybody is stupid.

You storm down the stairs out of the attic where you sleep in a makeshift room blocked off by hanging blankets. Through the bedrooms, into the dining room, into the kitchen, onto the back porch, slamming open the screen door.

Grandfather, who came to live with the family and built an apartment over the garage next to the house, stands in the driveway with an expression that says he is completely out of his element and has no clue what to do. Mother sits on the porch steps, again taking the abuse in her most humble and tolerant victim fashion. Devil is screaming at the top of his lungs. It doesn't matter what he's saying because you've heard it all before.

When the screen door slams open, everyone stops and stares. Beloved But Stupid Mother tells you to go away. You ignore her. Grandfather looks at you; finally, somebody who can handle this. But Devil, yes, Devil turns to you, points his cigarette-holding fingers and says what the fuck do you think you're doing slamming the screen door and —

He does not get to finish because you scream — yes, scream! It feels so good! — shut the fuck up you goddamned son of a bitch.

For a split second there is total silence as several things register in your consciousness. One: Little Sister and Baby Brothers are standing behind you in the shadow of the porch, pumping their fists in the air, and quietly saying yeah, you tell him, you tell him, you tell him.

Two: Beloved Mother is shocked you cussed because now that you're a devout Christian this was something you just did not do at all, never ever.

Three: Grandfather cannot believe you know those words and he is shocked, too.

Four: Devil is furious.

And here it comes.

What did you say to me, bitch, with major emphasis on *bitch*.

You scream it again, this time enunciating even more clearly just in case he's asking because he missed it the first time.

Shut. The. Fuck. Up. You. Gawd. Damned. Son. Uva. Bitch. Got that?

Oh, he got it. You cock your head at him at the words got that and Scared Mother says Honey is gonna kill you and you better apologize right now. Devil waits for an apology. You look from him to her, back to him. Shaking your head, you say there will be no apology. That feels so good.

Then you launch into a tirade against his stupidity, his reign of torture, and so forth. When you finish, he asks if you want to die. You tell him he hasn't got the guts to kill you just like he hasn't got the guts to pick on anybody stronger than him and he always, always, always picks on those weaker than him as you point to Weak Mother who is not happy you're pointing this out about her and you mention Little Sister and Baby Brothers, who are still doing a victory dance in the shadows.

You pause as you feel great! Invincible! Powerful! Devil does not move. Grandfather quietly goes up the steps to his apartment. Stupid Mother has that look on her face that says she has no idea who you are. You pull yourself together and say you're now going back to bed and expect quiet so you can sleep because, of everybody standing here, you're the only one with a goddamned job and you really do need your rest, thank you.

You slam the screen door shut, go back to bed, fall asleep with no worries, and only wake when the alarm goes off and you get up and go to work where you have peace in the noise of the spinning machines and the giant vacuums marching up and down the aisles and the repetition of pulling off empty cones and replacing them with full ones, and walking, walking, walking up and down the aisles thinking only of cotton.

It isn't until you're in your late thirties that Little Baby Brother asks if you remember that time on the back porch and tells you what he remembers. He said you were a force of nature and he loved you that day, though nobody ever mentioned the incident again and Mother never said thank you.

As usual.

Beloved Mother

There are only four pictures of your mother under the age of fifteen. But she doesn't have them. A relative in California does. There are very few stories you've heard about her early life.

The first story she tells about her early life is that her daddy almost catches her in the back seat of a car having sex with the man she'd marry and who is your daddy. Yes, she giggled, you were conceived in the back seat before they married. Tee, hee, da, hee, hee. Good times, yessss... She was seventeen when you were born.

She also talked a lot about sex with a bunch of boys in school from the time she was thirteen. She said she realizes now that she was considered the easy girl, the bad girl, and didn't even know it. When a boy asks if she's taking care of birth control, she asks what's birth control, and he almost faints.

Her parents never talked about that stuff and she didn't know to ask. Sex sure is fun, to hear her giggle about it and get that faraway look in her eyes. Unbelievable someone should like this thing that's used to hurt you. You study her and listen, and still she's a mystery.

She had once been very pretty. Vivacious. Energetic. At least, that's what the early pictures show. Pictures from when you were growing up show a beatendown woman, lacking sleep, worried, trying to smile when commanded.

So there she is, still having sex with Devil and having miscarriages, and yet things are so bad she eventually asks you to quit school when you're sixteen to fund her very last escape, and you quit, and then she gets pregnant again and swears she doesn't remember it happening because she was so tired.

Naively, you say you thought they were sleeping in separate beds. Her expression says you're kidding, right, and she never explains how she could get herself knocked up when you gave up high school.

Anyway, this child she carries to full term and you end up delivering him at home. Honey wakes you up and says it's time, come quick. She is having contractions and they are painful. What can he do? Get her some whiskey; she drinks four shots in a row and her body relaxes and she cries it's coming, it's coming, and you get her to the bed and get her clothes off and the new daddy sits at the side of the bed a total useless blathering, blubbering slob crying for you to make it all better.

You ask Mother what she wants you to do, but she's screaming in pain and pushing. You hold her feet and it seems to help and she keeps asking what do you see, what do you see, and you don't want to look at *that* but you have to.

You see what can only be the top of a little head and tell her. She asks if it is okay, and you say it looks fine and she screams what do you know about having babies, eeeeeeeeeeeeeeeeeeee!

You hold her feet with renewed vigor. New daddy blubbers and wails and pats her hand as he sits in a chair beside the bed and you watch the baby's body slide on out after much effort and screaming and you want to throw up and you swear you will never watch this again or have a baby ever because this is just gross. You help get the baby wrapped and really don't remember much after that; he is healthy, that you know, and he grows up and becomes a daddy himself to a fine little girl.

So, there you are, seventeen, delivering Baby Baby Brother and you're the same age as Mother when she gave birth to you and you think again: What an idiot. This will never happen to me.

Blubbering Daddy struts around town telling all about how he delivered his son and you have to hear the stories. No mention is made of your part.

Nicknames

There's always a preponderance of bad times in the family, but there is one thing everyone is good at: Coming up with nicknames. Grandfather named you Angie-Ah. It came about this way.

You were full of questions, always wanting clarification of your understanding of each answer. So whether it's why people lick watches, or learning to be a barber, becoming a major league baseball pitcher, practicing the long-honored art of massage, driving a straight-shift truck, wondering why Vienna sausages are so named as you eat them cold out of the can, picking and selling to neighbors fresh collard greens and spinach, or any other number of things Grandfather teaches you, he would at some point be unable to answer, simply ending with Angie…ahhhh, as he shook his head and rubbed a hand over his face.

So Angie-Ah was born.

You name him Hershey Bar and Beloved Mother commands you not to call him that; he loves it and tells her to let you call him what you want to call him, and she looks at you like how does she always manage to get her way?

Then came the naming of Little Sister. You're not sure who perfected it, though you suspect it's Big Baby Brother because he's very funny and witty and gets away with murder with Beloved Mother when he makes her laugh so hard as he walks away from the scene of the crime.

So anyway, here is Little Sister who is deathly afraid of worms, who constantly scratches her head in one spot until it is bald, and is angry with everybody. In general, she sets herself up to be the victim of more practical jokes than you can remember. One day Big Baby Brother says something about how she acts like a dodo bird and then out pops the name: Deeda-Leena-Lina-Do-Do-Bird. It drives her crazy and of course you all use it endlessly to her torment.

By the time you're in your mid-teens, Devil has taken to locking up his stash of porn. After all, Beloved Mother and you and Little Sister are good Christians now and while Baby Brothers go along for the ride, they still pick the lock when he is gone and enjoy the scenery within.

Big Baby Brother picks out a device in one of the magazines, the name of which he decides he'll now begin calling Little Sister. Double Dildo she is rechristened.

Somehow Little Sister knows what it is and goes insane every time he says it. You don't know what it is, but like the sound of it and laugh, and particularly like the show it starts. No amount of threats. No amount of begging Beloved Mother. Nothing will get Big Baby Brother to stop tormenting such an easy target.

But, Big Baby Brother hates his nickname, too. JoJo you name him, and he gives you a dirty look every time you use it, but what can he do? He can't supplicate Beloved Mother who he's ignoring on the same subject and he has to tread lightly with you anyway because you buy his clothes, the clothes he wants that Beloved Mother says he can't have. So he sucks it up and says nothing — and you both enjoy the little rebellion.

Little Baby Brother also goes insane when he is nicknamed. His father, Devil, who does claim him as his own, is French Canadian and has named Little Baby Brother something suitably French that just does not work in the North Georgia mountains: Michaelangelo-Dahhhhling.

Funny thing, though, it fits him. He is a little darling and smiles all the time and you like him best. You don't see it as an insult, but never call him that because his manhood is offended and you just can't do that to him.

Beloved Mother does not escape the naming. You have a cow in the pasture that has to be milked and the cow's name is MeeMaw. This becomes Beloved Mother's name that the boys will call her. She tsks-tsks each time and rolls her eyes in frustration, though by now you formally call her Mother.

Years later when you write your first children's book and dedicate it to your grandfather, and you're in schools talking to the little kids about the book's dedication and you understand the importance of making them laugh, you recite a funny version of the nicknames and tick off each one from Grandfather to Little Baby Brother, the kids laugh and chuckle and giggle and the name they like best is Michaelangelo-Dahhhhling and they always repeat it out loud and laugh some more and get the sweetest looks on their faces when they say it.

You tell Michaelangelo-Dahhhhling this story and he thinks it is funny that is the name they like best and now he isn't so mad about it anymore.

You Don't Have a Daddy

During your mid to late teens you make a few friends and these friends have daddies. You spend time with these friends and notice how they love their daddies and their daddies love them.

So there you are, quit school to work for Mother's escape, delivered the baby boy she went and got pregnant with that will delay the escape for another three years, work six nights a week and a lot of overtime, a good Christian girl, pay for a car you don't want, buy groceries you don't get to eat and clothes you don't get to wear, not one penny saved for the big escape, still running interference between Mother and Devil when called upon, and you're worn out and depressed only you don't know it.

In bed one evening, you hear the same old crap going on downstairs. You run down the stairs and tell everybody to shut up. Just. Shut. Up! They stare and shut up.

You grab your purse and keys and take off, to where you know not; you just drive. Soon you're at the house of your friend Brian. His mama and daddy are nice and you park in their driveway and stumble to the door in the dark and bang, bang, bang on the door with fists and when they open it they see a crying, doubled-over wreck, and the whole family drags the wreck up the steps and into the living room and they ask the wreck what in the world is wrong and the wreck cries out with all the heartbreak of having no daddy.

The mama and the daddy and your friend and his two younger brothers feel for you and the six of you sit in the living room in a huddle, their arms around you, crying for your loss as you pour out frustration and grief.

After their comfort, you stop crying, they walk you to the door, and you go home, still where there is no daddy, but knowing that if you needed one, Brian would share.

And One to Grow On

The day you turn eighteen, Beloved Mother becomes very unhappy with you. The conversation centered on, as best you can remember, the following theme: I'm a legal adult and you can't tell me what to do anymore. Definitely not an original conversation between a parent and a child, but this one comes about because all of a sudden Beloved Mother's acting like what she thinks a good mother should act like and you still disagree with her style.

Now she's trying to force it down your throat and acting like you're being rebellious and becoming a menace to society or something, which you are not. You're still working six days a week, with a lot of overtime thrown in, and being a good Christian and she's coming down on you like you're the one who jumped parole after getting out of prison after fourteen years and was molesting little children and beating her.

So, no, this isn't flying.

This conversation starts a few months before you become legal and comes to a head on the day of. It's loud. It's long. And Devil watches the show as if it is the funniest thing he's ever seen. He refuses to help Idiot Mother make her case because, after all, he's watching a twinkle side of you he's never seen and he likes it.

Idiot Mother's solution to the entire conversation is to threaten to spank you with The Leather Belt. Little Sister screams, yeah, beat her. Baby Brothers, thinking it would be very funny to see a now-eighteen-year-old adult get her ass whupped by Mama, can't drag their eyes away from the spectacle even if they think it's stupid.

So there everyone stands in the dining room. The words The Leather Belt hang in the silence. You turn to Idiot Mother and say, you're gonna whip me?

The challenge is out. Who will win?

Idiot Mother says she's still your mother and you will stand right there while she gets The Leather Belt. You tell her she can't make you but, seeing as how she thinks she's a real mother and all, you will stand right there and not move and wait for her to come back with it and begin the beating.

She stomps off to the bedroom and finds a huge leather belt. She doubles it up. She puts her hand on your arm to hold you. You shake her off and say do not touch me with your hand. You cross your arms. You turn your head toward your backside and tell her she may begin.

Eighteen times she whacks you across the backside. Granted, the first few are hard, but when she sees no flinch, and you don't blink, staring at her like she is nothing but a fly landing on and taking off from your butt, well, she begins to wish she never brought up the subject. But she can't stop in the middle and save face.

She continues on, getting easier with each swing, until finally she says and one to grow on, and delivers the nineteenth like this was a ha-ha funny whupping on a birthday or something, which it isn't.

You win and rub it in: Are you finished?

She nods, puts the belt away, the crowd disperses, and you go to your attic room to privately rub your butt and make faces because she's strong and she was swinging and it hurt, but damned if you will give her — hell, give any of them — the satisfaction of knowing that.

First Boyfriend

When you turn eighteen, a friend's daughter decides you need a boyfriend and that boyfriend must turn into a husband. The friend says her daughter is coming to visit and wants to get your picture, so dress up. You wear a dress you just made and hose and heels and put your hair up as best you can. You aren't smiling for the picture. The M-word has been used: Marriage. This is serious stuff.

The friend's daughter poses you and gets several shots and says she will send a picture off to the guy who is four years older than you and see his picture, isn't he handsome? You agree he is and you like his name and your friend and her daughter know him, so how wrong can you go, right?

A few weeks pass and you receive a letter in the mail.

Honey tells you about its arrival and wants to know who he is. You answer that somebody thought you two would make good pen pals. After all, he lives in West Virginia and it isn't like you will be dating him or nothing. Honey is satisfied and hands over the letter.

The young man is a good Christian like yourself, so he says. His letter is full of funny things and you like him immediately because he writes very well. You reply though it takes a couple of weeks to get it just right and copy it over so there are no mistakes.

Several months go by and letters are bumping up and down the road fast and furious. One evening the phone rings. Honey answers it, listens, says yes she is here, and turns and says it's for you. You ask who it is because you never get phone calls. Ever. He says it's your pen pal. You're surprised and Honey can tell. You go to the phone and, in front of everyone, have a conversation. Pen Pal tells you he is coming to Georgia and wants to visit. Take you out to eat. See the sights.

Come to the house.

Meet the parents.

Never in your life had you thought this would happen so you never planned how to handle it. Pen Pal arrives in two weeks. He goes to worship meetings with you. Takes you on long drives. In a little grotto he kisses you like crazy and gets aroused. You feel it. Oh. Hello there.

He gets it under control when he sees your shocked expression, but keeps kissing and you feel warm and fuzzy. You like the feeling but aren't sure what it's all about. He comes out to the house the next evening, brings a guitar, and sings songs for the family, all of whom except Honey stare at him like he is a creature from another planet. Pen Pal does his best to entertain and make everyone laugh, but nobody does. Honey does not like this situation.

So, Pen Pal puts the guitar away and pulls out two decks of cards and says he'll teach you a new game called Crazy Eights. Now this you all get into because playing cards and Monopoly and Scrabble are the only things you do together as a family…other than all the other junk, that is. The card game is a big hit. After it ends it is time for the Bicentennial of the nation's birth to be celebrated and everyone gathers in the living room to hear The Boston Pops play the 1812 Overture, Honey's favorite tune, and then watch the fireworks.

You sit on the sofa with Pen Pal. Mother's in a chair in a corner of the room. Little Sister and Baby Brothers are on the floor staring up at the television. Honey is in his naugahyde chair pretending to look at the television, but he can't keep his eyes from turning toward you and Pen Pal.

Honey can't stop looking because Pen Pal has settled back on the sofa, moved you to where you sit between his legs, leaned you back on his chest, wrapped his arms around you, and nuzzled you, sort of. Pen Pal gets all excited and bites your head and Honey's eyes get big; he doesn't know what to do because he never thought this day would come so he had not prepared for a boyfriend for Little Con, his own in-house twinkler.

A few months later Pen Pal breaks your heart, of course. No. That isn't true. You don't cry because you're sad he's gone. You cry because your ego's hurt. The details of his leaving you are so public. He has the rudeness to marry another friend of yours he'd been seeing at the same time. She knew about you, you didn't know about her, and when the friend who made the introductions tells you, your pride's hurt so bad you cry for weeks.

You see him about ten years later and know details of his marriage by then. You have two children of your own and are married. You tell him it's a good thing he married the other woman because if he had done to you what he did to her, you'd have killed him and he would be dead. He laughed at first. He stopped when he saw you were serious.

Their marriage is not a happy one and you feel sorrier for him than her because he got in way over his head by marrying into that family, and you're sure they let him know it all the time. The last time you see him, he's an old, old man, old before his time, and sad. A very sad man.

The Stroke

The family's in an uproar: Honey had a stroke. His entire left side cannot move, his mouth hangs slack, eye pulls to one side, arm hangs useless, leg is curled. He lies on a bed on the enclosed front porch. Unable to smoke, unable to speak clearly, unable to threaten anyone; quite simply the family doesn't know how to act.

His actions dictate the ebb and flow of each day. Silence in the morning as the household prepares for the day — Devil's sleep must not be interrupted. Silence in the afternoon upon arriving home from school — or hell to pay for interrupting his mid-afternoon nap in his easy chair.

So there he is. Unable to fool anyone that he's all powerful. Unable to threaten anyone in his weakness. Depending upon the graciousness of all who pass to wipe his drooling mouth. Lift him and give him a sip of water. No one thinks to take him to the doctor — or if anyone thinks it, they keep their mouth shut. Surprisingly, he doesn't ask to be taken. Everyone now must figure out how to manage their day without his input.

Quietly, Grandfather descends from his garage apartment and he, hated as he was by Devil, takes it upon himself to make Devil better. Twice each day he gives a complete body massage. From top to bottom — every inch of his extremities, chest, neck, back, feet — Devil can feel the powerful hands of Grandfather kneading his muscles and coaxing his body to circulate, circulate, circulate oxygen to the wounded areas.

Devil, hating to depend on the largesse of his father-in-law, at first condescends to the attentions. But after a few weeks, Devil feels improvement and, little by little, he's made whole.

For quite some time you do not believe Devil's sick. You think he's faking as he did when he went to die in the woods like his ancestors the Indians. And as he did when he pretended to be dead in his easy chair. He isn't faking this time, and you feel sorry for him as he watches you walk by each morning when coming in from work and each day on the way to running errands and each night leaving for work.

You see him moving his mouth and gesturing with his good arm for you to come near. Mostly you pretend not to see; finally when he can speak loudly and clearly enough for his begged commands to be heard, you can't pretend anymore. You approach and ask if there's anything he needs and if the answer's yes, you get it for him and help him eat it or drink it, but not smoke it.

Honey falls more in love and tells you each time that it's you, only you, who really cares for him and wants him better. And you nod and smile each time he says it. The nod and the smile hide your real feelings, the ones you can't show, don't dare show —

Die, you son of a bitch you, die.

He doesn't and Grandfather proves, as he wanted to, that massage helps stroke victims, and for years he talks about it to whoever will listen. This is one experiment in alternative health care you wish he never did because when Devil improved having learned nothing about human kindness or appreciating weakness, he was as good as ever at being Devil.

Unforgiven

So there's Devil, fully recuperated from his stroke after several months, and back into his usual swing of things. As if he has to make up for opportunities lost, it's now you are struck by him for the first and only time.

To the left side of the face a full, open-handed slap is delivered and finally you feel some of the same pain the others get. Your vision blurs momentarily. Automatically your left hand rises to where the warmth of his hand can still be felt, or maybe it's the blood rushing to your skin, you don't know. The warmth is a surprise. You didn't think of violence as being warm.

The early morning blow shocks and hurts Devil more than you. Big Baby Brother, standing behind you when it happens, waits for you to cry because by now he knows you're a girl, sheesh. But you don't cry. You simply face Devil feeling the warmth of his violence and stare at him with hand to face.

Devil doesn't know what happened or how to move forward. He takes a step back. He says…he says…something; you don't understand his mumble. He walks in a tight circle ending up facing you again, though the shock of his action is not lessened.

He asks why you made him do that. You say nothing. You feel the warmth of the violence going away. Big Baby Brother's expression shows he wonders about your not crying. After all, you should cry. You're a girl. You. Should. Cry. Beloved Mother and Little Sister cry. Why aren't you crying? You wonder the same thing. That violence against you stops what had been days and days of violence to the family.

Days and days of coming in from work and getting his attention and directing it away from Beloved Mother as she sat helpless on the sofa during his tirades. Or away from Baby Brothers who don't empty the trash can just right or stack the wood just so or milk the cow completely dry or whatever. Or away from Little Sister as she has her meltdowns and needs a good slap, though you let those slaps happen because she truly needs them to focus.

But after your slap an uneasy quiet, unlike anything the family has ever experienced, soaks the house and the day proceeds to move into late afternoon. And you know what's coming. You know Devil will turn into Honey and he'll come to you and beg you, once again, to forgive him, as he promises he will never do that again, whatever it is he thinks he just did on this day, and you'll smile and say you forgive him and he'll say he loves you and —

This afternoon, you sit on your bed, staring out the open window. You feel the breeze and smell the rain that's coming and immerse yourself in the sensations and think: He will not be forgiven on this day and never again.

And in walks Honey, Devil peeking out of his eyes.

And there he sits next to you.

And here he is taking your hand.

And now his head is bowed in shame.

And you watch as he does exactly what he always does and you wait for his words. And here they come.

Oh, baby, I'm sorry. I don't know what came over me and I love you, don't you know that and can you...

— Here's the best part —

...find it in your heart to forgive me?

And you smile and see the Devil calculating as he knows he's won you over again, and he's shocked for the second time that day.

No.

What did you say, bitch?

You tell him no again and he wants to know why and you tell him and Devil says your life will be more miserable than you can imagine and you smile bigger and laugh and say you knew it, see!

You feel light and free even as you know life will now get worse. But when he leaves the room, he is what you said he would be:

Unforgiven.

Michaelangelo-Dahhhhling

Little Baby Brother can't hear very well and for that everyone is grateful. By everyone you mean Beloved Mother, you, Little Sister, and Big Baby Brother. Little Baby Brother adores his daddy as all little boys should. And he goes with his daddy everywhere and talks to him non-stop which, of course, drives Devil mad because he can't understand a word Little Baby Brother says, is not inclined to try to understand, and thinks he gibbers.

The rest of you know differently. Little Baby Brother is telling Devil everything y'all do, and where, how, and when you do it. You know if Devil understood any of this, your lives would get much worse.

So when the day comes that Beloved Mother finds his hearing loss is because tubes are needed in his ears, his daddy is happy to have those fixed and Little Baby Brother comes home able to hear. Everyone understands the implications. How to handle this development?

Little Baby Brother doesn't want anyone to get in trouble. He is just a baby and doesn't yet understand his perfectly normal actions are gonna get the rest of you killed or beat. He has not yet learned to be sneaky. You all also know something else about Little Baby Brother: He'll never learn to be sneaky because he just ain't got a sneaky bone in his body, wouldn't know how to be sneaky and, furthermore, would almost view it as cheating. Little Baby Brother is a sweetie pie and as innocent as they come.

The family has a discussion about the problem of Little Baby Brother. It is decided each will protect him from any knowledge that, should he repeat it to his daddy, would get any of you or him in trouble. You also want him to enjoy his daddy because that is what he should be able to do. His daddy likes him, too, even if he does treat him bad with dirty tricks like telling him to jump from something high and he'll catch him and when he jumps, Daddy turns his back, letting him hit the ground, and other stuff like that.

It's a dance that's hard to choreograph, but y'all do it, and after a while it becomes second nature.

The fallout hurts Michaelangelo-Dahhhhling more than any of you ever realize. He always felt, rightly so, that each of you were keeping secrets from him and he couldn't understand why. Sometime during your early forties, Little Baby Brother asks why you hated Daddy. You stare at him: You don't remember? He says obviously not or else he wouldn't be asking the goddamned question. So you tell him, not all, but enough that he, as a grown man and father himself, gets the drift.

He tells you later he believes you more than he would have believed any other family member because you never lied to him and had never been mean to him. Though he hates what he hears and doesn't want to believe it of his adored daddy, he does believe it.

By this time, of course, his daddy was already dead, though Michaelangelodahhhhling often took a six- or twelve-pack of beer to the grave, cleaned it up, and sat and cried over him as he talked to him and asked why no one else cared for him now.

Now he says he'll never again waste good beer on that son of a bitch and never goes to the grave again.

You, who never went to the grave, get to wondering about it and the next time you're up to see Beloved Mother, you think you'll swing by and take a peek. The closer you get to the church beside which he's buried, the more fearful you get. You shake. Cry. Can't breathe.

Pulling into the church parking lot, you sit for a half-hour getting under control as you repeat he's really dead, he's really dead, he's really dead. Finally, getting out of the car, walking to the grave, you find the anger and scream every name you can think of as you kick the dirt around his sunk-in grave. When the anger's gone, you fall to your knees and cry some more.

Worn out but feeling great, you drive to Beloved Mother's house and tell her about it. She gives you the same look she always does: Who are you and where did you come from?

Because, you see, Beloved Mother does not understand at all why you're so mad and scared and emotional about this. She says it's her who got the abuse and now it's your turn to stare. Un. Be. Lievable.

After you leave Husband in preparation for a divorce, Little Baby Brother comes to visit the day after he reams you out for not visiting Mother in the hospital. You tried to explain that your visit would not be welcome and that Mother did not need an emotional drain on her health. He disagrees and says it's Mother, for God's sake, and you're her daughter and if she's sick she'll want to see her daughter so get your ass up here and he'll go along if you're uncomfortable.

Michaelangelo-Dahhhhling, such an innocent little sweetie pie who believes the best of people. You hate to disappoint him and say you will, in fact, drive up the next day as long as he'll go with you.

Three hours later he calls back and says not to ever again waste any goddamned gas money on that nut of a woman. He, who did not want to believe you but did because you never lie to him, went to the hospital where he had a great visit with Mother and she was happy. But just as he was leaving, he casually mentioned he'd be back the next day (she smiled) — with you.

Her one-hundred-eighty degree change of demeanor was immediate. Michaelangelo-Dahhhhling had never seen her like that, was horrified at what happened and, after arguing for an hour that surely she didn't really feel that way about her oldest child, now understood for the first time what you had been dealing with all those years. Instead of you driving up to see him, he came down and visited.

You two spend time together having conversations you both need to have. He begins to understand the family dynamics more and you bond with your favorite brother; a bond, by the way, that you need more than you ever thought.

JoJo

JoJo, or Big Baby Brother, rarely smiles. Kind of weird seeing as how he's so witty and funny and keeps Beloved Mother laughing all the time. When he's first in school, a teacher tells Beloved Mother she's worried about him because he never smiles even when he's playing hard. Beloved Mother comes home and says she doesn't understand why the teacher's worried. You do, and wonder why Beloved Mother isn't.

JoJo's daddy was always in question. Until he legally changed it, his last name was yours because he was born before Beloved Mother divorced your daddy; he wasn't your daddy's, that's known for sure. And though his name also reflects a French Canadian heritage, the name he's called every day was given to him because his real dad, according to Devil, was Joe D-, some guy Beloved Mother banged when he was out of town for a spell.

Beloved Mother never denies it, and it's a sore point that can't give JoJo a reason to smile. Plus, Devil tortures JoJo with full-head masks so scary that when JoJo sees them he screams and fights and runs to hide and often ends up behind the refrigerator in a dark corner as Devil makes fun of the crybaby scaredy-cat.

JoJo's fondest memory of you is him knocking you on your ass when you're thirteen and being so scared you'd kill him, he climbs a tree and stays there all day before he realizes you ran inside the house crying like a girl. He's never afraid of you physically again, and for a while took to sneaking up and hitting your breasts with his fists full of anger for Daddy. Large bruises and lumps and sore breasts. When you once run to Mother when you see him coming and get behind her and scream for her to tell him to stop, she pushes you toward him and says to stop complaining as he hits so hard you fall into the counter and can't catch your breath and think your breast will fall off. He never hits you again, it scares him so. But the lump of his anger remained painfully inside your body for a year.

When you move out of the house when you're nineteen, it's JoJo who takes it hardest. You remember him once asking why you left him. You explain it wasn't because you wanted to leave; you couldn't return or else your life would be more miserable. He never understood, and years later when you wrote open letters to the family to get some conversation going about your shared lives, he says it's all your fault his life turned out so bad.

He never does try to understand and the last time you talk to him he asks bluntly why you insist on calling. When you say because you're my brother and I want to know you, he coldly asks why. You're stumped. Why do you want to know him? You don't know why, can't come up with a good reason for knowing him, and until this day have never talked to him again except once accidentally when you answer a phone and he thinks you're Mother.

You're sad about JoJo, but realize he's a lot like Mother and Little Sister and there is no changing that. Still, you wish he hadn't been scared by Devil and wish he hadn't been beat with The Leather Belt and wish the wooden cutting board hadn't been broken over his back when he was nine.

Deeda-Leena-Lina-Do-Do-Bird

Little Sister's always a mystery to you. She's your complete opposite. Angry while you're happy. A real genius in school while on most days you barely get by. Always a victim while you're not. Envious, wary, and hateful toward you while wanting you never to leave her, always help her, and play with her.

She steals your things, not because she's stealing, she just thinks what's yours should rightly be hers, and in her mind it becomes hers so what's the big deal? She demands you do things for her and beats on you a lot. Yeah, you're stupid to have put up with it so long, but time just sort of got away from you. You did something about it — eventually. That theme of time just sort of getting away while you put up with other people's shit becomes clear one day, and you divorce and cut out other undesirables in your life and feel much better.

But back to Little Sister. You remember some good times. Playing Slap Jack at the dining room table and both yelling skunk at the same time and laughing and laughing because it's so funny you should yell skunk when you're playing Slap Jack. Counting and rolling the change from the bottom of Beloved Mother's purse and showing her how much she had for groceries so you could eat. Riding bikes, and skating, and swimming in the ocean and farting underwater and letting the farts roll up your backs and screaming Pepe le Pew when you smell them. Laughing in bed while she burps on cue and you make farting noises with your underarm. Working together at odd jobs and saving money and spending it on Beloved Mother so she'd have a few nice things.

You also remember the times she purposely tried to drown you and would've if you hadn't been stronger. Or the times she beat you. Or the times she tried to get you in trouble with Devil only he saw through it, thank God. And her pure hatred that began when you were in sixth grade that has lasted to this day because, she tells you some years later, you stole her very, very best friend and then she never had another one and it was all your fault. Or when she was furious at you for getting married before she did because she wanted you to wait until she got married before you could be allowed to be happy. Or...

And more and more and more and you hate to think about it and don't want to beat the dead horse so you stop the list.

The day you realize there's no hope for her, just like Mother, is the day your daughter sees firsthand what you'd been dealing with all those years and as you two drive home she says she has no idea how you survived it. That day is when you say you've taken all the first steps toward reconciliation you can take and only call Little Sister when Mother is in the hospital and say Little Sister is doing a fine, fine job of looking after Mother and to call if she needs help. She never does call, thank goodness. And she isn't doing a good job, either, but if you'd said that, well, Hell itself would have rolled down the mountain and she'd have another reason to hate you — and still nothing would have changed about Mother's care.

You are sad about Little Sister, and realize she is a lot like Mother and Big Baby Brother and there is no changing that, either. Still, you wish she had not been a victim and wish she had not been beat with The Leather Belt and wish all the smiles she gave Devil had done her some good.

The Square Dance

During your growing-up years in Atlanta, elementary schools taught square dancing. So when you move to Northeast Georgia and your congregation throws a square dance when you're eighteen, you're ready. Lots of young single men show up from all over, some from Atlanta. They won't dance with you, though quite a few of the other girls are asked and are dancing up a storm.

Sitting on the sidelines, you analyze. Why aren't they asking you? You look at each face lined up against the opposite wall, many of which have eyes turned toward you, and see the exact same expression on each:

Fear.

You understand now how to help others with their fear and form a plan. Your goal: To dance a lot that evening. Your method to accomplish said goal: Be the asker, not the askee. Your action plan: Get up, start at one end of the row, and keep asking until someone says yes. To your surprise every one of them says yes and the whole evening is spent asking, dancing, thanking, and repeating with the next young man in the line. In between dances you scan the faces again. You see expressions change.

If they had danced, they are smiling and hopeful. If they had not, they are fearful they will not be asked, but seeing you make your way down the line asking each in turn, short, fat, tall, ugly, or handsome, their hope shows through the fear. You feel good that these young men — most of whom traveled such a long way to come to the square dance — will leave with good memories, all because you simply wanted what you wanted: To dance.

Still, you left the dance and wondered about that for quite some time. Why had they looked at you with fear? Why could they not face that fear and overcome it? Why did it have to be you who had to pretend she had no fear so others could be comfortable or have fun? Years later, after your divorce when you go out dancing, you see the same thing: Fear. And again you are, for the most part, the asker, not the askee, though now you get turned down more than you get accepted because the men are shell-shocked from years and years of life and so forth. But all you want to do is dance.

Sheesh. Boys.

The Cigarette Man

After you moved back to Georgia from the North Carolina Escape From Devil that didn't last but one week for Mother, you didn't want to go back to the cotton mill and work third shift. You had been working first shift at McDonald's in North Carolina for three months, and sleeping at night was just the best thing ever. So you moved in with Grandfather, who by that time had moved from the garage apartment to a small house near a post office.

You and Little Sister share a room. With your hatred of clutter and needing to have some sort of order to the house, you take Grandfather's stuff and move it all around until it looks nice. He comes in and gets upset with you for moving his stuff and you stand there in your twenty-year-old confidence that you are right, and tell him you will not live in a place with such...such...well, you just didn't have the word to describe the mess and will not let Grandfather live like that either.

He starts to say something, then shakes his head and says Angie...aaaahhhh, and walks away. He later says he thinks his house looks mighty fine now, less like the inside of a garage storage area. You smile and cook him a spaghetti dinner and he chows down.

So, there you are, no job, got to find one and somehow it makes perfect sense to drive down the mountain, past the State Patrol station where you got your driver's license, and up into the next town, to look for a job.

You find one at a convenience store. The same store where you get robbed at gunpoint, twice, and where you meet the man who would later become your husband.

Before you met him, you meet the store manager who hires you on the spot. You know how to use a cash register, can talk pleasantly, aren't bad looking and, besides, you don't mind working second shift, nor do you mind working on prime date nights, Friday and Saturday.

He can't figure it out. You tell him it's quite simple: You do not date. This he finds unbelievable. He asks if you're a virgin. This is the first time you've ever been asked that and, technically, you think you may have been, but don't know for sure; still for all practical purposes you feel that if you aren't, you hadn't given it away voluntarily, so therefore…

You say yes. He nods his head and says okay.

Manager was slim, short, with long blond hair, wore his pants tight to show off his assets, and was popular around town. He soon quits flirting with you when his charms don't work. Not long after, every guy in town's coming into the store, buying beer or rolling papers or Mad Dog 20/20, and asking you out on a date.

No. Nope. Not gonna. Forget it.

You give no explanation and, because your answers are always delivered bluntly with a severe face, no one asks a second time.

So one night, about two hours before closing, the cigarette salesman comes in. He's taller than you, long dark hair, good-looking fella, tells funny jokes, and doesn't ask you out. Just talks. He walks with you out to the pumps to get the gas readings. Helps you stock the shelves. Yaks it up about his hometown and other stuff. Then you fill the refrigerator cases and he's right there in them with you.

You remember what you wore that night because this is the first time you remember a man commenting specifically on your clothes. You wore a thin polyester blouse with flowing sleeves, gaucho pants, a bra and panties and hose and chunky high-heeled shoes, platforms they called them.

So, there you are, both in the walk-in fridge when he says he sure can tell you're cold. You are not cold and say so. He says sure you are. You ask how he knows what temperature your body is. He says, almost bashfully, well, your nipples are showing.

Nipples showing? You look down and, sure enough, there they are bigger than life and you say, huh, how about that? Then you look up at him and he smiles and you say that's a reaction to the cold in the fridge, and you really are hot. He agrees you are, indeed, really hot.

Then you get confused. Hadn't he already said you were cold and he knew it? Now he says you're hot and he knows it? You finish with the gallons of milk and invite him to step out so you can close the door. Then it's time to count the money and drop it in the floor safe and lock up for the night.

Cigarette Man says he sure is hungry and don't you want to talk some more? You agree you're hungry, too, and sure you can talk. So he says you can ride with him in his car to Waffle House, where you had never eaten though you were a Southern girl. You get in and off you go to Waffle House, where he buys you food. A first! Or a second. You can't remember for sure. No. Wait. It was the second time. There was that time West Virginia bought lunch. Oh, yeah, and you went on a date with one man in North Carolina during The Great Escape From Devil. Okay, so three times. North Carolina is nice and when you tell him you aren't going to have sex with him because you aren't that kind of girl, he says he does not think you are and then you kiss and it's nice.

Anyway, for three hours you regale Cigarette Man with stories from the Holy Bible, stories, of course, he is completely fascinated by. It's almost three in the morning and you sure do have to get home, so can he please take you back to your car? This was such fun, you say, as he drives away from Waffle House, past your store, and into a parking lot up the street.

He parks. He gives what you now know to be a come-hither look. You stare and before you can get out your question, he leans over, puts his hand behind your neck, and kisses you.

Well, you're so surprised you don't know what to do, but out of habit, because after all you French-kissed Devil goodnight every night for years and years because that's what you had to do, you automatically kiss Cigarette Man back though you aren't aware that's what you're doing.

You pull away and ask what the heck he's doing.

He whispers for you to come to his hotel room.

What? You aren't a whore, you tell him definitively.

He leans back against his door, puts his hands up, and says he didn't say you were. He likes you, he wants to show how much he likes you, and you say you don't need to know how much if it means going to his room.

He puts his hand behind your neck again and again you kiss him back. You pull away again and tell him to stop. He asks why, since you're kissing him back and you swear you are not doing that at all. He kisses you again and you kiss him back. This time you pull away and ball up a fist and say do that again, I'll kill you.

He is confused and rightly so. You keep your fighting fist cocked and never take your eyes off him as you say to take you to your car. He shakes his head, starts the car, and when you get to your car you tell him to wait, you have something for him. He smiles big.

You get out and go get a book and bring it back to him.

Here, you say, read this. It will explain all about God.

You slam the door and never see him again.

The next day Manager comes in and he's laughing his butt off and saying you're the first one ever not to go to bed with Cigarette Man. Both Manager and Cigarette Man are impressed even if they are frustrated.

You go through a large part of your life oblivious on so many levels. No wonder so many men end their conversations with Angie….ahhhh.

The Bet

Manager sees your virginity as an opportunity for making money. You don't know that until one day a young fella comes in and lets that little fact out of the bag. He asks for a date. You say no. He says he knew you'd say that, but he sure hoped to win the bet. Stopping short, his eyes get big. Oops.

What bet? He doesn't want to tell. You repeat with death in your eyes: What bet? He caves and tells the whole tale. It seems Manager, who is one of the playboys in town, tells all the other guys he knows of a sure-enough virgin girl who will not give it up no matter what. In typical man fashion, someone says oh yeah, wanna bet, and the bet is on. There was a lot of Manager's money riding on you not losing your cherry before you got married.

So from September until you quit in March, the store does a brisk business, mostly male, as you say no over and over. But now you know about the bet and tell the boy he can just pass the word around that you're hip to the bet and you'll make sure Manager knows you know, too.

Does that stop the bet? No. Now it just gets more fun. How can she be asked to go on a date and yet think this isn't part of the bet? The strategizing that went on had to have been fun to see. You don't know about that until later, though, so you just get madder and madder every time someone asks you out. You're still mad when another man asks you out. No, you tell him bluntly. He wants to know why. You tell him he has long hair and smokes and he isn't a Christian like you and —

Whoa, he says, I ain't asking you to marry me, I just want you to go to a party. You give it to him with both barrels blasting and he leaves, then returns and gives it right back. That gets your attention.

Against Mother's wishes — the one and only time she's ever been right — you end up marrying him almost five months later. You'll be married thirty-two years and have two children together before you leave.

He didn't know anything about the bet.

Becoming Obedient Wife

Until you married, you rarely needed permission to do anything. You supported yourself, even if it was from paycheck to paycheck. You made the decisions that guided your life. You got your GED.

Then you marry who you think is a good man and, in truth, he is, but you're messed up and he's messed up and you both don't know it. Your gut told you, it screamed at you, not to marry him, and you ignored your gut because — and this is key — Mother agreed with it and Mother's always wrong.

Husband would've been a nice guy to work for. He would've been a great guy to help move some furniture. He was not the best husband for you. Still, you would not take action on that conclusion until thirty-two years had passed and every nail in the coffin lid of the marriage had been driven home.

So you marry and set your mind to becoming the best obedient wife you can be. You study the Holy Bible and the Holy Bible says good wives are obedient. Yeah, you learn much later that some people twist it around and lord it over others, but at the time Husband smiles, buys you lunch, follows you home from work late at night to make sure you get there safely, and says he's going to become a good Christian like you and does.

Okay. So your gut's screaming, Mother's pitching a fit, and you're ignoring them both, even after the honeymoon. Even after the first child is born. Even after he tells you to leave if you don't like it, though you can't take the baby. Even after the second child is born. Even after he continues to tell you day after day after day you are not good enough. That you do nothing good enough. That you are not smart enough. That you never are obedient enough.

And he isn't happy with you and doesn't smile at you anymore. And you have no money and have no say-so and must ask permission to do anything at all, even if he is at work.

And you cannot figure out what you're doing wrong. You study the Holy Bible more. You talk to other women who offer hints and tips on making a man happy. You know how to analyze, study, and apply to reach a goal, and yet it isn't working.

So you ask permission to do everything because God said good wives are obedient and you are bound and determined to be good. You will be good, damn it. You will be good. You are not a whore. You are not a slut. You are a good wife. A *good* wife. A *damn good* wife. Lots of people tell you so. Lots of men want a wife like you. So why doesn't Husband see it?

After some years, though, your confidence is gone. When your real personality does pop out occasionally everybody likes it, except Husband and Father-In-Law and Sister-In-Law and Brother-In-Law and Mother and Little Sister and Big Baby Brother.

You read in the Holy Bible that you will be happy if you are obedient to God and God wants you to be an obedient wife, so why aren't you happy?

You're smiling. You're laughing. But you aren't happy and the darkness gets worse and worse until one day you break.

And Husband forbids you to break. You cannot stop the breaking and disobey him. Then he forbids you to tell anyone you are broken. You have to get help to be put back together and tell him you must disobey again. Then he forbids you to take medicine that will help with being broken. Again you disobey.

And you ask yourself does God understand that you're broke and must disobey Husband and you find out God does understand, and better than any mortal, so you stop asking Husband's permission to fix the break and just go about the business of doing it. And Husband likes the results, though only for a little while. He sees you getting better. You do one thing you wish now you had never done. In the belief that knowledge is power, you tell Husband all the ways you are broke and why. You regret sharing those details and it becomes one of the catalysts for a long-overdue divorce.

Still, you know God is right. Obedience is not a bad thing and when a man is a good husband, your obedience will be a happy thing because it will not be used for selfish reasons and you, who have discovered hope and happiness is still alive within you, look forward to the day a good man as mate will smile at you and think you're the cutest little thing ever and ain't he just the most fortunate guy in the world to have such a smart wife and all the rest of you idiot men who passed her up can just eat his dust.

Devil Dies. Honey Dies.

You're married and three months pregnant with your first child, a daughter, when the news comes. Little Sister calls long-distance from North Georgia to south of Atlanta where you live.

He's dead! He's dead! He's dead! She does nothing but scream this over and over in a most ecstatic fashion. Of course, you're expecting the call because for the last twenty-four hours Still-Scared Mother has been constantly calling.

He wants to see you. You must come. He's dying. He wants to see you. He told me to make you come. You don't understand, if you don't come I'm gonna be in trouble. You must come. Phone call after phone call the answer remains the same: No.

Devil's obsession with you never diminished. After Still-Scared Mother tells you Devil's coming to your wedding no matter what, you send a message through Still-Scared Mother that if he shows up you will have him carried out bodily and call the police and have him arrested.

He knows you do not make idle threats and never shows up but holds hostage the knife you used to cut the wedding cake. You insist Still-Scared Mother get it and bring it to you. When she finally brings it, he'd hurt the blade somehow, and you tell her he is to buy a new one that looks exactly the same because you will not accept this piece of trash.

She looks at you like she always does: Who is this person and how am I related to her and where did she come from?

You get your new knife. Still, when you get pregnant, and if it's a girl, you're afraid he'll come and hurt her, and you're frantic with worry for your child. So it's not unwarranted that you don't want to put your child near him and, besides, you stopped responding to his commands a long time ago and aren't about to start again.

Especially since he is open-quote-dying-close-quote. Hadn't he played that game too many times to get you to show something toward him? This is just another ploy.

Still-Scared Mother seems to believe he's dying, but what does she know? She believed him plenty in the past and she's always wrong. Still, he died. Died begging for you. Will wonders never cease?

So when the call came you screamed and threw the phone and Husband rushed into the kitchen and picked it up and heard he's dead! He's dead! He's dead! And he hung up on Little Sister. You keep screaming as you bend over double, holding your unborn baby and crying and Husband sits in a chair and puts you on his lap and rocks you for an hour until you stop shaking and crying.

He doesn't understand though, and says he's sure you will miss your stepfather and you look at him and say are you an idiot? Miss him? Miss him? You wanted him dead and scream again; this time it's mixed with laughter of relief that your baby is safe, safe, safe. You keep repeating that to yourself and it is comforting.

But, you have to see for yourself he's dead and the next day you drive to North Georgia and Mother's house and then to the funeral home where he's laid out in fine fashion. His older sisters, believing Catholics, not Atheist Catholics like their brother, moved from New York to live near him in their final days. They're crying and praying on a prayer bench next to the coffin.

Widowed Mother stands at the head of the casket greeting fellow mourners — you have to smile at that — and she takes to her role well. You walk to the casket, smile, and look at everyone in the room. You laugh loudly; everyone stops and stares.

You laugh again and point at Devil in the casket and Husband asks what you're laughing about. You get the laughter under control and tell them.

Ha, ha, this is his best joke yet. He's messing with your minds. He's gonna be awake in a couple of hours, heck, he's awake now, just doing a good job of faking death like he always does.

You think this is classic and can't believe how good he's carried this out. Husband looks at Widowed Mother and shrugs what does she mean? Widowed Mother walks over and says Devil's really dead. You keep laughing and shaking your head no, no, no, until finally you're hysterical in the belief he's faking. Widowed Mother says they already sucked out his insides. He's really dead. You get more hysterical. Husband tells everyone he's taking you away. They agree it's a good thing.

Later, Little Sister's running through the house shouting inches away from everyone's faces he's dead! Little Baby Brother is threatening to kill her with his big knife if she doesn't shut up about his daddy. Big Baby Brother is smiling and can't stop smiling and brings an egg over to Husband and says here, I bet you can't break this by pushing on both ends, and Husband falls for the joke and gives it his all and the egg breaks all over him and Big Baby Brother laughs while Husband cleans himself off.

Little Baby Brother flicks his knife open and shut and cusses while you and Widowed Mother serenely gaze at the wild but normal scene as Baby Baby Brother, only four now after coming along when you were seventeen, plays on the floor not knowing what's going on.

And Husband is having a meltdown. He takes you into another room and says he has to go back to work the next day and he's leaving. He would prefer you come with him. But the funeral is in two days, you say.

He wants you to come with him now. You do not understand and he cries. He's scared. He's never seen anything like what he's seeing in there — he points dramatically — and he doesn't want his child in harm's way. Your suggestion that you can stay at a friend's house doesn't help calm him and you walk out to Widowed Mother and siblings and say you will be going home now.

Widowed Mother is not happy you aren't going to the funeral. She says what will everyone think? You say you don't care. Husband has requested something and you shall honor his wish. Surely, Widowed Mother, you understand that concept, right?

Widowed Mother doesn't know what to say; you leave the madness behind. Because you didn't see Devil planted, you believe that somehow he is carrying this joke on. One day, when your daughter is almost two, you're in the grocery store and a man who looks exactly like Devil is in the line next to you and he turns to you and smiles and you scream, grab your daughter, leave your cart full of groceries, and run for your life. You get home and lock every door and window and pull down all the shades and draw the curtains.

This begins a long period of panic attacks and fear of going out without Husband so you get very, very busy being the best cook you can be and figuring out ways not to have to go outside without Husband. He sure does eat as well as possible on a limited budget and with what his mama brings to put in the freezer.

But the curtains stay shut…in the house and in your mind.

A Girl Child is Born

Each time you have a child, which is twice, easy technology does not yet exist that will let you know the sex of the child and you aren't rich, so you have to find out when it is born. So you pick out names and none of them work and Father-In-Law suggests a name and you both hate it and try others; still nothing works as a name for your first-born.

Then around seven months pregnant, Father-In-Law suggests the name again and this time you both like it and the deal is done.

Of course, having birthed a baby brother, you swear you'll never have children. After being on birth control pills for seven months, and these almost killing you and you coming off of them, and allergic reactions to condoms, Husband tells you not to worry about getting pregnant because The Pill lasts in a woman's body for a long time.

You say you think he's wrong there, because the docs pretty much said not to miss a day or else. He says he's been married before and knows these things and you're Obedient Wife and the condoms hurt, so you don't worry. When you go to get fitted for a diaphragm, they say you don't need one.

Yay, you think, you're deformed and can't get pregnant, but well, surprise, surprise, you're nine weeks along. You call Husband at work to tell him — he who also didn't want children and to this day swears he didn't, though you pretty much know for certain he did or else what's with the stupid story about The Pill, right? Either way, at the time he says nothing and hangs up.

When he hangs up you know you'll be kicked out of the house because he's been firm about not having kids. You cry the rest of the day and await his final determination of your fate.

When he arrives and sees you crying, he assures you he is not going to kick you out and is happy about the baby. You aren't so sure, but he smiles, so…

You call Mother and tell her about her first grandchild. You ask how to get in touch with Daddy. She does not know. You make calls until you find out about the Armed Forces World Wide Locator service and send off a letter.

The doctor says to sign up for birthing classes. But why? Because a nurse midwife will be delivering the child if all is well and you have to know how to help her. You shrug, though for the life of you, you do not know why you need practice. You're sure you will not be birthing no baby, and that is that. Obedient, though, you sign up.

Classes start. Pillows are brought and a room full of pregnant women with attentive husbands sit on the floor in a circle. Week after week you learn about breathing and timing and pushing and contractions and stuff you will never need to know. You humor Doctor and friends and Husband because they say this is necessary.

One day in class, near the time to go to the hospital to have the baby, you don't practice the exercises. The teacher says you really must. You look at her, wide-eyed and innocent, and announce you will not be needing any of this. Teacher looks at Husband, who leans forward and says gently as if talking to a young child: Yes, you will.

Adamant, you restate your position. Every woman shrinks back. Every man puts his arms around his precious wife who is being good and practicing and they all babble that yes, indeed, you will need this stuff.

You look at Husband with the full knowledge you'll never once have to time a thing, nor will you have to breathe like that. They still give you a certificate of completion and it is official: You are allowed to have the baby. So, what with one thing and another happening that signals birthing time is near, you end up at the hospital and unpack in The Birthing Room. After a few hours and nothing happening, you hear a woman screaming down the hall. You recognize the scream; mother had one just like it — eeeeeeeeeeeeeeee!

A nurse asks if you'd mind leaving for this other woman. You pack and wait in another room. The other baby is born, the room is cleaned, and you're brought back in. Several hours go by; another woman comes screaming down the hall. You move again. She births, they clean, you move back.

It's been twenty-four hours or so since your water broke, and still nothing is happening. They administer drugs — and nothing. They wait and wait and wait — and nothing. Finally the decision is made for a c-section.

They take you in to prep for surgery. You will have a spinal injection so the baby will not get any drugs in its system. They ask if you feel any pain in your toe and you do. They wait and ask about the toe again. You still feel the pain. They wait and ask again and still you feel the needle. You hear someone say she's ready and don't know how they know you won't feel any pain.

During all this, of course, you're telling one joke after another and the doctors and nurses can hardly get the room ready for the procedure because they're laughing so much. Husband's washing up in the other room and will sit at your head. So Doctor comes in to operate and Husband is mad because everybody's laughing while his baby is about to be born and the doctor and his helper doctor are talking, talking, talking about golf and the lake and a bunch of stuff and you're ready to get this show on the road.

You keep asking when they're gonna get their butts in gear and get that baby out. They answer politely, for a while. Then the head doctor turns to Husband and says she sure is a bitch at which point you're ready to jump off the table at him but can't move and Doctor says to put in your order: What do you want? Boy or girl?

He pulls out the baby, who is screaming and mad and pees all over everybody and everything, and Husband stands up and exclaims.

And your daughter is born without all the mess of blood and pain and screaming. Clinical and clean and organized, that's how you like it.

A few days later you say to Husband, see, told you we wouldn't need the breathing and timing. He just shakes his head and you get busy trying to figure out this girl child in front of you.

A Boy Child is Born

The pain of the c-section was doable, though you don't want to repeat it and tell everybody you will not have another child. Two years pass and Brother- In-Law's wife gets pregnant with an oopsie. It will not do that his child should be the youngest grandchild in Husband's family. It will not do at all. Husband doesn't say, but he's upset his brother might get more favor.

So you tell Husband, the baby of his family, you want another child and he says he won't help the process, but he won't stop it either, so if you get pregnant it will be your fault. Whatever that means, you think, and get busy. You have a false alarm one time and think you're pregnant but aren't and you cry and cry. Then the day comes when you know you're pregnant. There's no doubt in your mind or body.

The doctor's test says you aren't and you tell him he's wrong. He shakes his head and says to get another test next month. Still not pregnant, says the test, but you know. Finally, both exam and test confirm you're as pregnant as you thought you were and you can't wait to tell Husband's daddy that Husband will have the last grandchild of the family.

Birthing classes are ordered again, and again you know they will not be needed. When it comes time to let the baby out, the doctors administer drugs again and still nothing happens and you say told you so and they take you in to prep for surgery. Doctor's chair breaks while he's giving the spinal and you cry and say he's broken and now he can't get the baby out and he stands in front of you and bends this way and that to show he is fine.

You tell more jokes, but by now Husband knows it's you making them laugh and soon Husband is told to stand and he gets to watch and —
It's a boy!

He won't breathe, he's turning blue, he looks very serene, nothing like your daughter, a screaming hellion until she was eighteen months old just because she wanted things her way. Breathe or not, I'm okay, his expression seems to say, but they get him to breathe and he pinks up and they bring him to you.

He puts his nose on yours and you rub noses and from that time until he is five, when he is hurt or sad, he wants to rub noses for comfort and when you do it, it is as if you're comforting the you at that age.

Whereas Daughter was a dainty eater and never made a mess and you couldn't hear her nurse and nobody knew she was under the blanket unless you told them, Son swallows loud and sucks hard and stretches out the nipples searching for more milk and gasps for breath and screams because even when he empties out both boobs (you can say those words by now) in record time, he is still ravenous.

So now you have a daughter and a son. And you vow again to be the best mother ever and continue to attempt to make Husband happy even though it seems like that will never happen.

Your kids, they hug you, and they kiss you, and they smile at you, and you laugh with them; with them you get a little bit of the happy childhood you never had.

And when your grown son and daughter, now a mother herself, say you did a great job of being their mom and they love you, you cry because, while you may not be able to feel love yet, you did your best to show it when they were growing up and you hoped and hoped that when they got grown they would have felt love from you and could say good job, Mom.

And they can feel it without flinching.

And they can say it without lying.

Daddy Leaves You

So you sit at Daddy's graveside as he gets a twenty-one gun salute, and stare into the eyes of a soldier holding the flag over his coffin and the soldier can't take his eyes off you as you fight harder than you've ever fought not to cry and your body shakes and the wind of the Texas winter whips through Ida Lou Cemetery cutting you to the bone as you listen to Widow cry, and Little Sister and the two half-sisters cry like they miss him and even Husband's crying and he didn't even know the man who abandoned you.

You refuse to cry. You will not cry. And this soldier has to help you not cry so you never stop looking at his eyes and shed not one tear. No, you will not miss Daddy. You refuse to miss him because your little-girl wishes never came true and dreams for Daddy died a long time ago. Today is a mere formality of his absence from your life.

But when Taps begins you think you'll have a heart attack and the soldier's eyes get big when he sees the control you're exercising and the shaking of your body and he is told twice to fold the flag; he can't take his eyes off yours because you hold him so tightly.

Beloved Mother sends you a condolence card. You call to say thank you. She says she's sad, too. After all, he was her husband once and the father of her first two children. You brightly tell her it's no big deal. After all, you never knew the man, not really, so no skin off your nose. You're fine. Just fine.

Really. Fine, fine, fine.

You're already divorced when Daddy's sisters tell you stories you hadn't known about your early life, Daddy, and Grandfather and Grandmother on Beloved Mother's side.

Now you really don't like Mother anymore because everything they tell you is the truth and it fits with little bits and pieces of self-serving stories Mother told. The version that made Daddy look bad for no good reason. Daddy, who was going to come get you and keep you when Beloved Mother was gone for that year when she left you with Grandfather and Grandmother and nobody heard from her. When she found out Daddy was coming, well, that just wouldn't do and she got there first.

And now you cry for Daddy and those tears feel good. Then the tears begin to hurt because you're angry at Mother. Mother, who you will never believe again no matter what she says. Mother, who slowly, almost imperceptibly, stopped being beloved some years ago.

The Banishment

When your children are small and you're living near your in-laws where you moved to help out Husband's family, several things happen within eighteen months. Your father visits and brings your two half-sisters. Your father dies. You travel to Texas for the funeral and during the weeklong trip Husband realizes there is something wrong with you and you almost die. Your children both almost die from burst appendixes, three months apart. Other medical dramas happen during this time and you're overwhelmed but smile, smile, smile because that is your habit.

So when offers of help come from Mother and Little Sister, you're grateful, so very, very grateful, and you, always the one to bear the brunt of the pain, feel such warmth in your heart for Mother's and Little Sister's help that you let your guard down.

It is in that letting down of the guard, though, you find out what they are truly like. Their offers of help are just that: Offers. Carry-through is worse than non-existent until finally you do something you didn't think you would ever do.

After having been told they'd bring dinner, you find the unprepared food piled on the kitchen counter and they tell you to cook them a meal while they play with the kids. And you, who are used to dealing with pain, walk to the kitchen, crying.

When Husband arrives home and finds they've added work for you, he is furious. You tell him to say nothing and he doesn't. You set the table and call them in to eat. Everyone sits. Husband prays. Amens are said. Mother and Little Sister wait for you to prepare their plates. Mother and Little Sister get up and get dessert and give it to the kids. You tell the kids to eat their food first and dessert can be had when they finish.

Mother sniffs, righteously indignant, purses her lips disapprovingly, and sweetly tells the children they don't have to listen to you. Little Sister, unmarried and not a parent, begins to lecture on the proper etiquette of looking after a husband and being a good parent. Baby Baby Brother, in his mid-teens at the time, stares into space and you cry again.

Husband says nothing and in his silence Mother and Little Sister smell approval and become ever more disapproving. The lecturing continues.

You can't breathe. You get up from the table in pain and, doubled over from crying, leave the room. Husband doesn't follow, but Baby Baby Brother does and pats you on the back and says he understands, he understands, pat, pat, he understands.

You get under control and Mother and Little Sister, who have a long, long drive home of at least thirty minutes, say they have to leave and you're left with the dishes after they pack up the leftovers and take them.

A couple of days later you write the letters, one for each, wherein you state definitively they are never to darken your door again until they can come in and treat your husband with respect, be nice to you and, furthermore, visit with the children in the living room, not in the bedroom behind closed doors, what are they trying to hide anyway?

Mother calls and says she understands. She was abused, too, you know, for years and years. She was forced to do things she didn't want. She knows you're married to an evil man who's forcing you to write these horrible letters. She doesn't hold it against you and offers you a place to live. Quick! Quick! Throw the clothes and kids in the car and come live with me, she says. You're astounded. What world does this woman live in?

You tell her Husband doesn't even know about the letters, that you wrote them, you mean them and, furthermore, don't call ever again. Yes, yes, she whispers, he's standing right there, listening to you, she understands. Wait until he goes to work and sneak out.

You hang up and laugh, not because it's funny. It is a semi-hysterical laugh full of relief at never having to see them again. Of course, you're wrong and they manage to make life miserable a few more times and try to damage your reputation with lies they believe are true because they — oh, never mind. You know what they are.

Memories in the Boxes of Your Mind

The problem of not remembering never occurs with the stories of your life. It's always the little things you forget, like your name or how old you are or where you are or which grade you're in or how to add and subtract. You know, the little things one does not need to know to live. The things that, should they be forgotten, no one will die.

The first time you don't remember doing something, you're seven, hiding out in Florida after the nonprofit arson, and a man who lives next door comes over to complain about you. He hates doing it because he thinks you're as cute as a bug in a rug and sweet, too, but it just won't do to write in the dust on his car because it might scratch the paint.

Honey calls you over. Little Sister follows. The man says hello like he knows you; you don't know him. The situation is explained. It's your name written in the dust and since Little Sister doesn't know how to write and you do, it has to be you who wrote the name. Did you do it?

Eyes wide, beaming pure innocence that is not faked because you don't know how to fake that for yourself, you look at Honey and say you didn't. The two men look at each other, at which point the decision is made to show you the deed. The four of you walk to the man's car. Sure enough, there's your name in your handwriting; how did it get there? You shake your head and say you don't remember doing it. And they believe you don't remember.

The man, nice as can be, and Honey, gently, both say it's okay this time, but not to do that ever again because it can hurt the paint. You nod and promise and the nice man goes away. For the next forty years you experience the same situation over and over.

We met at the business meeting, you gave such a wonderful speech...

You aced the math test and are the smartest kid in school...

You knew how to divide yesterday. Why don't you know how today?

I thought I told you... Why didn't you...?

It's very important that... Don't forget to...

At waking, you always know two of three things: Where you are and who, but not why you're there. Or why you're there and where there is, but not who you are. Or why you're there and who you are, but not where there is.

It's a miracle you manage to function productively day to day; that is, you keep a job and are a valued employee, then raise your children well, and people depend upon you to be on time and get things done.

Still, memory aids don't work. If you meet a woman with a flower for a name, you will call her Lily — even though she's Rose. But that's genetic. You get it from Mother.

Mother Confesses

After some years of attempting to understand and please Beloved Mother, you no longer care whether she approves and when that day comes, it is as if she is dead. You do your duty by her as the oldest of five, call occasionally and check in and one day she says you ought to visit and you do. This happens about ten years before you get divorced. As you're riding in her car she says there is something she needs to ask. Have I...ummm...have I...ever apologized to you for your life growing up?

You answer: No, you have not.

She says she apologized to Little Sister and Big Baby Brother and Little Baby Brother, but not Baby Baby Brother because his daddy died when he was just a little thing and he never got abused. She's apologized to them. Okay. You wait for your apology, and she says she has learned something about herself and it isn't pretty. I am weak, she says. I always have been and always will be, there is no changing that. She looks for a reply.

Yes, Mother, you tell her, you know that.

Mother is shocked and asks how you know. You say you've always known it. And that is the end of the conversation and all you will ever get out of her; it never changes how she feels about you or how she treats you or that she'll never understand you or be proud of you or love you or...anything.

Because she is still jealous of your twinkle, now kept under wraps as much as possible, she insults you — sweetly, of course, as she still believes there is something wrong with you, not her.

That is as good as it will ever get and by now you know you'll be fine and never begrudge the woeful apology.

Then one day, after the divorce, Ex-Husband calls and when you hang up you're furious and sad at the same time.

Furious at his still trying to manipulate you, sad because the next thing has just become very, very clear: You married your mother.

No wonder she recognized it wouldn't work.

Knowledge is Power

When you have your big old meltdown and go to therapists to try to figure things out, you come home and explain all to Husband. He listens carefully and before you know it, you're calling him Doctor because he gets almost as good at helping you through bad times as they do.

You never forget how brilliant he is at helping you control the unlocking doors in your mind and dealing with the fallout. And you will always be grateful because his help was beneficial.

But, there comes a time when you get things pretty much straight, are ready to be happy and move on. Then something else happens, too. At the same time you no longer need a doctor as husband, you realize you need Husband to be a husband and it was time he was able to relax and do that. But he doesn't seem to want that.

So some drama ensues whereby you read him the riot act against crappy husbands and he pretends to try and that gets you to shut up for a few years while other drama happens with his sick mother, and Daughter marrying, and grandchildren coming along, and such as that.

He wants you to stay weak. He wants to stay in the role of All-Knowing Doctor. He wants to stay as Savior. Why did he want that? Oh, it was so he didn't have to look at himself, his shortcomings, his foibles, his emotional sicknesses.

Why don't you stay in your role as The Big Helper and let him feel good about himself? Oh, that's easy. You're sick and tired of being insulted. It feels good to stand up for yourself.

So, there you go, Husband, find another woman as good. Go ahead, Husband, shove out the best thing you ever had. Go on. Be stupid.

Hey, you, enough of that talk now.

Bitterness does not become you.

Daughter and Son are Told

There's drama with the kids. Both almost die and surgeries save them. Son disappears one day when he's five and you cannot find him and run to the neighbor frantically calling for help and who answers the door but your boy? He's having hot tea and a chat which you don't mind, but you cry and the neighbor says she asked him if he had permission to come over and he said he did and he's been visiting for months and you, thinking the worst about who might have taken him, almost have a meltdown.

Schools are attended and relatives die, including the daddy you stopped wishing for but got in touch with right after his first grandchild was born. You almost die because by now you hide pain so well nobody knows you're sick. You move a few times, settling in the Atlanta area.

You finally have that big old meltdown and can't work in the schools anymore because the flashbacks are so bad, but you know you must earn money because Husband has said until you earn a lot of money you will not have a say in any financial decisions. So at the beginning of the big old meltdown you think this would be a fine time to start a business.

And you make money and make some more and Husband likes the money but doesn't like your attitude, because to go into business you had to disobey him and good wives God likes didn't act like that, but you do it anyway because you seem to know God pretty good by now and don't think He'll mind. Then the kids grow up and grandchildren come along and by now you know the marriage is over and are scared to death to officially end it, though you can no longer stay. Your biggest worry is for the kids, both adults; you don't want to hurt their lives.

You first tell Daughter you aren't sure where the marriage is going and she says do what you have to do and don't worry about her and her family. You are relieved she knows she can get along without you. You tell Son next and he says you have to be happy, Mom, and you cry. Both say they don't know how you lasted as long as you did and you cry more because you know that if your children are this clear on the matter, then nothing was exaggerated in your mind and the leaving will be a good thing for you.

Now you must tell Husband.

Husband is Told

You're going to tell Husband in January but get attacked by two big dogs in your driveway while the first half-black president is being sworn in. So after getting over the attack, in February you sit down in the living room and say you must tell him something: You don't want to remain married.

He tries to act surprised, but can't. Some discussion ensues and you tell him it is up to him whether you stay. He says nothing and you wait. You check back with him in March. He accuses you of having another man and you say you wish you had a man because you sure could use one, and he doesn't have anything to say to that.

In April and May and June and July and August he does something different each month that drives another nail into the coffin of the marriage. You begin a letter and finish it in a month. You put it in his chair at the first of September and read a book while he comes in, sees the envelope, changes his clothes, comes back, picks it up, reads the front of the envelope, sits in his chair, opens it slowly, and reads.

The letter is twelve pages long, detailed and clear. You hear sheets turning one after the other and count them silently so you will know when he gets to the end. You will be ready for whatever he says. He says nothing. He folds it, puts it back in the envelope, gets up and goes to bed.

You've already moved into the other bedroom and behind closed doors that night sleep peacefully because you are happy. Two weeks later he calls your bluff, only it isn't a bluff and he's too blind to see it. He writes a letter and pushes it under your bedroom door. He can't take this anymore. You must come back to his bed or get out. You end up moving out faster than expected and to do it spend more money than planned. That isn't what he envisioned.

Everybody you know is shocked, but not for the same reason. Some are shocked you waited so long and are happy for you. Others are shocked you did it. A few people take his side and you don't care because you have to start life over and those people were his friends anyway and by now you don't care what anyone else thinks about your life since they aren't doing so hot with theirs.

Husband still thinks you're carrying this a bit too far. He thinks you'll see how rough the big bad world is and come crawling back, of course, having learned your lesson — just as Devil thought you learned the lessons he was always teaching.

It seems Husband forgot all the times he told you that if you didn't like it, you should leave. And he cannot believe you left the big house and the big office you had in it to live in a thirty-five-foot travel trailer, so now he knows you'll really be back, bringing the travel trailer he always wanted, of course.

Before you move out he will make sure you can't touch his money and you both go to the bank and split up what is there. He asks you to sign away your interest in the house and you say all that will be handled shortly.

You give him a list of everything. Some things he gets, some things you get. His list is much longer because most of it is what he wanted in the first place. He is mad he has to buy out your half interest in the already-paid-for house; you don't need all that space for tools and project cars and room after room of furniture, so he gets the house. You patiently explain the financial benefits to him of this arrangement and, after he gets over his shock and talks to a few other divorced men, he realizes you did him a big favor even though you don't owe him one and he knows why you don't owe him.

The day you stand in front of the judge, you can't stop smiling and Husband can't believe you're taking it this far. The chatty judge asks if you want him to shut up and just make you divorced. You answer yes, sir, please, sir. He looks at you and you're twinkling again and he smiles back, signs the paper with a flourish and says you are divorced. You thank him and wait for the final papers at the courthouse. You have them in hand within thirty minutes and mail now Ex-Husband his copies.

You celebrate with an ice cream cone as you sit in the sun and smile and think about your next move. You will buy a place of your own and it won't be near Ex-Husband and it won't be near Mother, two people who previously couldn't stand each other but are now simply the chattiest best friends ever, allied against you, the common enemy.

You buy a small condo a little bit north of Atlanta in a vibrant little city full of music and writers and creative people and you fit in and people like you and you make friends and have big adventures and go dancing and write songs and try, try, try to make money with your business even though the economy is bad and worry your butt off about making it, but your place is paid for and pressures are small compared to many people's.

Then one day a light bulb turns on in your brain and you cannot shut it off so you turn on the computer and write and before you know it, your story to date is told and you are clearer about your life when the writing is done.

Let the Twinkle Shine

So here you are. Divorced, and happily so. Living near movement and life and music. Adventures come your way and men love your twinkle and tell you so. Devil-men still approach but you don't have to manage them, you just have to tell them to go away, and do so with a smile and a little wave and they can't figure it out.

Each of the good men, all of whom at this time aren't ready for you, unknowingly teach you something and you learn lessons Daddy would have taught you about men had he been around.

And you stay busy with dancing and immersing yourself into life, life, life, and yes, drama comes and drama goes, and you don't know what the future will bring but you know this:

God loves you.

You still don't feel His love and don't feel love for Him, but feel yourself getting closer to Him and isn't that a good start?

And you pray to your Heavenly Father and tell Him everything and know He totally understands your heart and know that no matter what the end result is for your life that this daddy won't leave and will do right by you, on that you can depend.

You tell God everything, leave nothing out, and ask Him to help you again be that happy child like when you were born.

And He hears you.

You know He does because you feel reborn, and you twinkle happily.

Afterword: 2020

A song by Robert Clark "Bob" Seger called *Against the Wind* has these lyrics that sum up well my journey as told in this book:

The years rolled slowly past
And I found myself alone
Surrounded by strangers
I thought were my friends
I found myself further
and further from my home
And I guess I lost my way...
...I began to find myself searching
Searching for shelter again and again
Against the wind...
...I found myself seeking
shelter against the wind

Twinkle — a memoir did not include many of the vignettes originally written. You see, I was looking for evidence of God's love and so I chose to write of the events that included demonstrable proof that God — even if I had questioned Him — was there and thus would always be in my future. Therefore, I did not see that while the emotional journey I had taken to the top of my little "Blue Ridge foothill" was for others the equivalent journey of climbing Mount Kilimanjaro while wondering if the volcanoes were going to blow. To top it all off, not a single clue was provided in order for them to prepare for that journey. I started suddenly, almost impulsively, and fully expected folks to casually follow along to a good ending they could not have foreseen.

Gut punches came too fast.

Another surprise kept coming my way, too. People said, "Wow. That was powerful. When are you going to write your follow-up and tell us about the rest of it?" My answer was always the same. "I can't quite yet. I need to live a bit more to have something to look back on and figure out."

Sorry to say, I'm not yet at that point where I can write a full memoir about the journey because it is still incomplete. Happy to say, this afterword may help bridge that gap. As of this writing, it has been almost seven years since the first penning of the book. Much has happened that took my attention; no need to go into any of that now. However, by now you will have noted that I had a deep longing for a mother who loved me. To this day, that has not happened with Mother. But another surprise was in store. Detailed in the upcoming section entitled **Healing**, it let me know my Heavenly Father is still watching because He sent something so good I could not have foreseen it.

Friedrich Nietzsche wrote, "That which does not kill us, makes us stronger." Ol' Friedrich sure did love his all-or-nothing statements. I hate all-or-nothing statements because, while there is a nugget of truth in each, they are usually factually incorrect in the bigger context, the context that matters. The fact of the matter is "that which does not kill us" can keep one weak, can foster the comfort of the victim mentality, can make one fail to see Truth and/or act on behalf of Good.

There can be no sacrifice unless the stakes are high.

Was I willing to take actions that sacrificed?

What were my sacrifices?

My sacrifice was my reputation. Here's why.

Against all the destructive messaging I got, messaging that wanted me to believe I was bad, I did not feel I was a bad person. Every now and then came positive messaging that supported my belief I was a good girl.

Which would I believe: The lies or the truths? But which were lies? Which were truths? One destroyed my reputation and the other gave me a good reputation within my own mind. Was I fooling myself when believing good about myself and attempting to reject the negative? Or was I truly the bad person Mother said I was?

My good reputation was a big deal because it was all I ever had that was mine and I wanted to hold on to it. I found out as an adult that even God defends His reputation against slander and other character assassinations. But I didn't know that as a child. All I knew was that to defend my reputation meant not offering myself up as a sacrificial lamb, letting Mother and siblings be hurt.

So my definition of "good girl" became limited on two fronts. One: By not being like Mother. And two: Ignoring God's hand in a matter because I listened to others when they said that God couldn't possibly mean *that*, whatever *that* was at any given time.

Some said they believed God was not limited, but they were mistaken because God deals with each human where their specific limits are. Which means God Himself lives with self-imposed limits. So, when I finally understood that God did mean exactly what He wanted me to understand, *that* allowed me to take action. Action that for most people might not work. But God met me where I was, giving what was needed in order to know Him best that I may be of best use to Him.

Do I believe? Yes, I do. More so than ever do I see His expansive hand…and I do not mean in a "pie in the sky" kind of way. One can say that when Almighty God goes against popular opinion, He Himself is putting His reputation on the line. That is a sacrifice He made that I will not squander no matter who disagrees or does not understand.

I have stresses, true, but my life turns out well. There are fewer barriers between me and my Heavenly Father now. Trust of Him has grown. I more quickly accept His guidance and see the good things He sends my way. When my ideas don't go as planned, I fret much less and not nearly as long.

Life and business on hold while I looked after my Aunt Pearl (more on that later), here I am again, exploring my continuing journey. To do that, I reread *Twinkle*. Besides what I mentioned in the introduction, my second response was this: Wow. Who is this person? Have I changed? And, dare I say it, improved? Well, let's just stick with change and assume that change is for the better, okay? Must stay positive.

Rereading my memoir, I made notes on the inside back cover of topics as needed exploring.

But how to organize these so that the telling was logical and not meandering hokum? There are three things that affect every person on earth at all times. They are: Nature. Nurture. Free Will. What are the effects of each?

Nature is our inherited traits. Passed along to us through DNA. Over which we exert little to no control. In this instance I speak not of the physical but of the character, personality, temperament, disposition, spirit, and humor of a person. Mother used to always ask, "Who are you? Where did you come from?" because my character, personality, temperament, disposition, spirit, and humor were so unlike her, her other children, or her mother. Obviously, other than having a physical relationship, she didn't know my father very well or she would not have asked such questions.

Nurture is that which we receive from others and, in a bigger sense, eventually learn to do for ourselves. Nature will always direct how Nurture is processed, thus making psychologists' and psychiatrists' jobs harder since one rule cannot apply to all equally.

But the foundation for the other two is *Free Will*. It can modify those so that even if Nature wants us to do X and Nurture says X is a good thing, Free Will can say, "Hey, Nature! Yo, Nurture! Listen up. You're both wrong. I forbid you to do that."

Or Free Will and Nurture want us to do Y but Nature recoils from Y. Or...well, you get the drift. Only we can decide which is strongest and will have the most say in any given situation. Which is why our Heavenly Father is so patient with us. It is only through His undeserved kindness that we have a chance. Which brings us back to me.

Abuse, especially incest because of the sexual nature of it, often produces in certain children a sense that they are all-powerful. I was no different. You see, according my stepfather, he only did what he did to me because I was so, so very cute. Oh, how I tried hard not to be cute, but it just didn't work, so therefore my cuteness was exceptionally powerful. My mother, on the other hand, looked to me from the time I was two-and-a-half to save her because, you see, only I could save her, an adult, from another adult.

That is heady stuff for any child, but especially for someone with my particular temperament. I grew up with an inflated though highly inaccurate assessment of my power. Yet that inflated assessment did, in point of fact, often save my mother and siblings.

Because adults told me I could, I did.

They were not surprised because, you see, they believed it about me. Still, because my temperament is one of questioning and confirming, major irreconcilable differences abounded, causing much confusion in this little girl's storm-tossed mind. A mind that can only get to the shelter that could be found in the love of Daddy, my Heavenly Father.

But how to get to that shelter and allow it to protect me?

Question. Compare. Question. Validate. And question and accept.

So, here I go.

Courage and Cowardice and Wisdom

The Apostle Paul said, "If possible, as far as it depends upon you, be peaceable with all men." *Romans 12:18*

And so I worked at peace awfully hard. But after trying everything to get along and heal wounds, those efforts did not work and staying away became the better part of valor. It took more courage to stay away from family. My slow reaction to taking a stand had to do with my reputation. What would people think when I don't visit Mother? Yes, the family talked badly about me and inferred much evil or lack of care or whatever it is they wanted to infer. Staying away meant letting those slung stones and flung arrows fly but simply not being where they landed.

Paul said "if possible". He also said "as far as it depends upon you".

I did my part but could make no headway and, no longer willing to suffer for no good reason, simply did not call or write to them anymore.

Many years ago, early one morning, Little Sister called and asked if I would go with her to a psychologist. I readily agreed. She then said, "Great! The appointment is in an hour." Well, I had a sick kid at home. I couldn't go then and explained that to her. She became furious and accused me of not ever caring for her. I explained over and over that I couldn't leave my sick child and asked if it was possible to go the next time she went.

The answer was emphatically No. And she never forgave me for not going with her right that minute to solve all her problems. In fact, when I asked about how her sessions were going, she said she quit because it was obvious that I didn't care.

Then I began talk therapy with a psychologist. When she asked how long I saw this process lasting, my reply was quick and definitive: Three weeks. She simply needed to answer my questions and I would be fine. Her reply was slower but equally definitive: Well, it usually takes as long as it takes. I popped back: Right. Three weeks.

Wrong! I was with her for one year. But during that time I proceeded to do something my family was not used to…or at least it appeared they were not used to. I spoke of secrets. Secrets kept from each other. Little Baby Brother had been kept in the dark for his protection. I did things the rest of the family didn't know about. Little Sister and Baby Brother remembered nothing of their childhoods. Mother's memory was…well, we'll talk about that later.

I'm a writer. Thus came the bright idea of writing "open letters". Simply telling them my stories of growing up. Each would get the same letter. All mailed on the same day.

Here's my next surprise: They all talked to each other...or so said Mother because next thing you know I'm getting a short chastising letter and a phone call from Mother relaying all the angst that had been dredged up. Everybody was mad at me because, she said, I was accusing her of being a bad mother.

Now, I'm hurt. I am hurt bad. So, okay. Is that how you want to play? Then it is on, and I fired back with open letter number two wherein I recounted the phone call and letter from Mother who was speaking on their behalf and then proceeded to add to the letter more history and how open dialogue about shared history would be beneficial, blah, blah, blah.

Baby Brother calls and is furious at me for attacking Mother.

Little Baby Brother calls and says it ain't helping so I should stop it.

But did I listen? No! I was in therapy, see, and it was helping with my life. Couldn't they see this was good for them? Boom! Letters three, four, five, six and, if memory serves correctly, seven flew through the USPS like heat-seeking missiles full of healing and love.

Only they weren't. What a self-righteous prick I was. In 2019, copies of these letters turned up in my file cabinets. I was particularly dismayed at how clumsy I was in approaching the subject with my family. No wonder they got mad. But then again, they were mad at me even when I didn't bring up anything, sooo...

After awhile I realized that Mother and siblings were not going to change and that I had to stand up for myself. Funny thing, though, is that the very husband I divorced (and who himself did not want to and would not transform) is the same one who gave me the ability to see my family clearly. He first gave me permission to tell Little Sister to take a hike. Shortly after we married, I was taking Little Sister around town to pay her bills and get her errands done. She didn't have a vehicle. After an hour of her screaming at me in the car, I put her out on the side of the road and told her to walk home.

Oh, Lord have mercy on me. Hell rained down from Mother and Little Sister about that. While I cried at the drama, putting her out of the car and driving off made me feel a power I had never felt before. I could say no.

I.

Could say.

Was allowed.

Had said.

No.

And lived to tell.

Hard lesson to practice and Husband encouraged me to do it. But when I started saying no to him about his subtle but nonetheless ever-increasing abusive ways…well, don't you know that would not do?

My cowardice, on the other hand, continuously haunts me. Obviously I acted cowardly when I hid in the hallway and watched as the cigarettes were brought out and Mother was threatened with being burnt when I was eleven. I did not step in at that time. I kept watch, but hid, not throwing myself between Mother and Devil. That night I could not make myself do anything for her. Why? Because I was too worried about myself. That emotional reaction was so strong that for years when I did not "step in" and "rescue" I went through days of beating myself up.

Step in and rescue who, you ask? Well, this is where the emotional reaction training become a weakness. It could be something as simple as two strangers sitting in a restaurant having an argument, but I just turn my head.

COWARD!

Yes, that simple. Nothing life-threatening in and of itself. But the emotional reaction was as strong as standing in that hall berating myself for not saving Mother from the threat of being burnt. I've had to work so hard to overcome this. As soon as it appears I've done so, up pops another opportunity to scream at myself.

Surprise! You're still a coward!

That internal message, along with one other (You are a slut and only good for one thing!), have been the hardest to overcome. I keep setting myself up to practice having courage. But one does not have courage. One can only act with courage when the time comes.

Speaking up or not is, of and by itself, neither courageous nor cowardly. Doing them at the right time, though — deep breath — takes wisdom. Wisdom I continue to work on having. Prayer is involved. Of course. And being open to receiving in a timely fashion the answers He sends. Definitely.

Without wisdom one can swagger or one can be cowardly. But wisdom pushes cowardice aside and supports courageousness. Wisdom teaches that silence is often the right thing.

Sibling Update

Little Baby Brother and I talk regularly on the phone. We get together and share a meal and have nice visits. We found we have things in common, like singing. Even if he did go astray for a bit, he is still the sweetie pie he always was, wishing and hoping for peace in the family before he dies. If he could have our mother and all his siblings in one room at the same time and it be a good, fun, happy visit and remain that way, he could die a happy man.

What he doesn't understand, and never will, and what I've come to a peace about, is this: That happy-happy will never materialize. In his heart of hearts he knows it, but he tries to ignore the reality because it makes him sad and he doesn't like to be sad. Recently Mother invited him to the house to have lunch with Little Sister. He called and reported that everybody was on their best behavior and it was a nice visit — even though he tiptoed around subjects he wanted to talk about. In any case, I was happy for him.

Yet the last time Little Sister, Baby Baby Brother, Mother, and Little Baby Brother were all in the same room with me — a restaurant — nobody had a good time. Our cousin had come to visit me from California. It had been years since she'd seen her aunt, my mother, and she really wanted to see as many relatives on our side as possible while she was here. I recommended that she call Mother and make the arrangements and that if Mother didn't want me to be there, I was happy to drive her up and get lost while she visited.

Cousin said that would not happen. Either we all visited together or she wasn't going to see them. Cousin called Mother. Mother was excited. Arrangements were made to meet at a Mexican restaurant in Helen, Georgia. Baby Baby Brother brought his wife and young daughter as well.

There we were. Sitting around the table. Everybody happy to see Cousin and get to know her. Cousin is asking questions and Little Sister pops out with a story. Everybody was laughing and I added some interesting and fun details. Cousin and Little Baby Brother laughed along with me, but Mother, Little Sister, and Baby Baby Brother and his wife all stopped laughing and turned their heads away. Then Little Sister sniffed self-righteously, frowned in my general direction, and said, "I was not talking to you." The three nodded in agreement.

Cousin couldn't believe it. Little Sister then turned to Cousin and began smiling and laughing and telling more stories, but Cousin had a very difficult time from that point on. The meal was tasteless.

After about an hour or so, it was time to adjourn. I said I had brought my camera that had a timer, and a tripod, for a group picture since we were all together with Cousin. After more drama, I finally managed to get everybody in one place, set the timer on the camera, clicked the shutter, and went toward the group. Mother said, "You're going to be in the picture, too?" I barely had time to answer yes and set my face in a smile before the shutter clicked.

Cousin was hugged and everybody said goodbye to her. Only Little Baby Brother spoke to me and I was again studiously ignored by the rest. I put my camera and tripod in the car and waited for Cousin. We watched everybody drive away and got in the car ourselves. I started shaking and crying. Cousin was furious and had plenty to say on the way back to Atlanta.

As of this writing, that was the last time I saw Mother, Little Sister, and Baby Baby Brother, or my sister-in-law and niece. In 1993, Baby Brother, who lives in New York state, made it clear he didn't want to hear from me because it was obvious I didn't care about him since I moved out of the house and left him when I was 19. But then around 2001 or so, he was making the Georgia rounds and brought his new wife and his daughter from a previous marriage to see us.

His wife had an opportunity to quietly say to me, "You aren't anything like I expected." Then she smiled. Encouraged, I made another phone call to him just to have a quick how-ya-doing chat and got from him, "Why do you call me?" When I said it was because I loved him and wanted to talk to my brother and keep in contact, he made it clear not to do that anymore.

Around 2016, I got a phone call from Little Baby Brother who wanted to know if we could ride together to New York for the wedding. I asked him what wedding. After some discussion it became clear that I had not received an invitation to the wedding of Baby Brother's daughter. Little Baby Brother was furious and said he was going to get me an invitation or find out why I had not gotten one. No amount of begging him not to do that would stop him.

A couple of hours later he calls back. Cussing. Furious. He was not going to the goddamned wedding since I was not invited. But he asked me a question: Have you been excommunicated from the church?

I laughed, said I had not, and wondered why he would ask. He said Baby Brother said I was not invited because I had been excommunicated and he knew it for a fact because Mother and Little Sister said so. Little Baby Brother called Mother who confirmed that yes, Angela had been excommunicated and they were good Christians who did not associate with such a bad person who had turned her back on God and…

Well, didn't that just bring back memories of living in Red Oak and having Devil excommunicate me from the family when I was thirteen-ish?

I'm telling you all this to say that I cannot report on anything definitive with the family. I'm telling you all this to say that I'm getting depressed just writing it. I'm telling you all this to say nothing will change with them and nothing can be done to change how they think about me or treat me.

I'm telling you all this to say that I now better understand the Apostle Paul's advice in *Romans 12:18* when he talked of the limits of one's influence.

Nothing I can do will make them love me, want me, care for me. To try to push myself upon them does not bring peace. They are grownups. They are responsible for their own actions. It is easy to believe them when they say they do not want my company. And I honor their right to say it and no longer try to force myself upon them in the guise of "family healing".

I have finally, thoroughly, accepted my limitations with my family.

And it is so freeing.

Mother: Memory, Delusion, Mentally Ill, or Evil?

For some years, Mother worked at a popular hotel in a tourist town in the mountains of Georgia. My husband and I wanted to go to that town and so I called Mother to find out if there were any openings on the dates we needed. There were. We arrived and checked in. The next morning her manager said to me, "You must love your mother very much. She is so kind and helpful and sweet."

"*My* mother?"

The manager seemed confused at my response. "Your mother is [Name Here], isn't she?"

I jumped through hoops to explain away that reaction and made a funny joke out of it. The manager laughed with me and all was well. Still, in my entire life I had never had anyone come up to me and say my mother was kind, helpful, and sweet. In fact, nobody ever had an opinion about her one way or the other that was said in my presence. This was a first and my response was truthful from my experience with her. But a public insult was definitely not kind to her and I went out of my way the next couple of days to happily chat at the counter, give her a hug or wave, and "talk her up" to the staff.

The effort wore me out.

Fast-forward fifteen years or so. My divorce was over and my granddaughter came to stay with me for a week during the summer. I wanted to take her to that town and spend a couple of days since the last time she'd been there she was barely four. I had heard that Mother no longer worked at the hotel, so I felt safe in calling and not getting her. She answered. Shocked at hearing her voice, I stumbled a bit over my words, but finally got around to checking availability. She tapped at the computer and asked —

"Will this be for one or two?"

"Two."

"Will you want one king-sized bed or two queens?"

"Whatever is available will be fine."

After more clicking around the screen, she then said, "What name will this be booked under?" I gave her mine, along with credit card info, and the room was officially booked. I said thank you. Then she said —

"May I ask if I am speaking to my daughter?"

"If you are [Name Here], then yes, you are speaking to your daughter."

"Ah. I see." And she hung up.

The reader is probably thinking, "Man, that is some kind of weird exchange." And the reader would not be incorrect. But what the reader needs to understand is this: Mother recognized my voice immediately and I knew it. How? Because her voice changed from professional hotelier to the righteously indignant mother I was used to hearing. Therefore, here is the exchange again with added notations in italics:

I had heard that Mother no longer worked at the hotel, so I felt safe in calling and not getting her. She answered *professionally, confidently, kindly*. Shocked at hearing her voice, I stumbled a bit over my words, but finally said I was looking for availability on particular dates. She tapped at the computer and *after a long inhale through her nose, asked in a clipped voice* —

"Will this be for one or two?"

"Two."

Exhaling through her nose, *that is in a quiet snort of disapproval*, "Will you want one king-sized bed or two queens?"

"Whatever is available will be fine."

After clicking around the screen, she then said, "What *na-a-a-ame* will this be booked under?" I gave her mine, along with credit card info, and the room was officially booked. I said thank you. Then she coldly spat out —

"May I ask if I am speaking to my daughter?"

"If you are [Name Here], then yes, you are speaking to your daughter."

Slight pause then a *harsh little laugh*, "Ah. I see." And she hung up.

I had the phone on speaker so my granddaughter could hear me making the reservation. We were having big fun, excited about the adventure. But after Mother hung up, my teenage granddaughter looked at me, eyes wide with shock. She said, "That was Grandma [Name Here]?" I nodded and she blurted, "Oh. My. God. I bet she thinks you're bringing a man!"

Granddaughter was more correct than she knew.

Then she started laughing and I started laughing and we went and Mother wasn't working while we were there and she had not told anyone her daughter was coming and I didn't have to worry about anything, so yay for me.

One thing is guaranteed: Mother probably does not remember that at all. Memory is an interesting thing. While I remember experiences and specific events inside the family and can put these in an autobiographical form (times, places, and other information that gave the memory context), my knowledge about what happened outside the family was limited.

For instance, I was six years old, sitting on the floor almost under the ironing board. Mother was ironing. The TV was on. We were watching when suddenly Mother burst into tears and screamed "No! No! No!" She was inconsolable.

Her crying and screaming were not unknown in my experience. I thought when she reacted like that, it was something only happening within the family and did not conflate it with anything else. It wasn't until I was an adult with children that I realized Mother was crying and screaming because John F. Kennedy had just been assassinated.

My episodic recall was highly accurate and served as the family's memory. For instance, I reminded them of consequences if chores weren't done. They did not remember those penalties — and were always surprised when punishments occurred. It was I who remembered that when Devil held his hands like *this*, *that* bad thing would happen. Seeing that in time could mean a heads-up to Mother and siblings, hopefully sparing them a beating or other torture. It was I who cataloged the emotions of each person. If I arrived late, that is, after the family had missed all the cues and shit was hitting the fan, it was up to me to read the scene, putting two and three together to get five, and come up with a way to stop it...or at least soften the outcome.

To say that the family's episodic memory was almost non-existent is not off-beam. On the other hand, their semantic memory was awesome. They knew what was happening in the outside world. Drugs, sex, rock 'n' roll, wars, social movements, and popular culture were unknown subjects to me except where they influenced the family. I had not heard about a certain war until the day it was ending…and only found out about it when seeing the entire family huddled around the TV, horrified, shocked, crying, and wringing their hands while watching the last dramatic evacuations on that helicopter. What the heck is going on? Years later that same footage was shown in a documentary. I blurted out, "Wow. That was the Vietnam War?"

Sometimes these lapses in my understanding were comedic. Baby Brother used to call Little Sister "Double Dildo". Other than Mother who went "Oh!" and hid her eyes, everybody laughed when she went insane. But, me? I simply stood there with the equivalent look of "Whuuuut?" I was married many years before I knew what a dildo was and still didn't know what one would do with it. That's when the husband looked at me with "Whuuuut?"

In another example, Mother completely prohibited fourteen-year-old Baby Brother from wearing certain necklaces popular with men at the time. She said only druggie hippies wore them. I was not aware of this ongoing and loud conversation and took Baby Brother shopping for clothes. He saw a necklace and asked my opinion of it. Well, I liked it on him and he asked if I would buy it. He seemed very eager to get it. I wanted him to be happy and this would make him happy, so pennies were counted, and it was purchased. He put it on and we got home.

Mother went ballistic and ordered him to take it and the new shirt off.

Baby Brother pointed at me and said I had purchased these for him. Mother wanted to know why the purchase was made against her wishes. I said I had no clue about her opinion on the matter. Mother and Baby Brother stared at me. I had completely missed this discussion because the opinion about the necklace had nothing to do with the safety of the family. It was a disagreement between two people who were not going to try to kill each other. Obviously any noise about that had gone in one ear and out the other and never stuck around for a moment in between.

When I was around fifteen, as Mother and Little Sister and I were studying the Bible together, Mother made a comment about how our childhoods were so great and she was so happy about that. Little Sister and I stared at her. She looked back at us and said, "What?"

There is no need to go into the whole conversation here but suffice it to say she was very upset when reminded about how she ordered me to do things to her husband so she wouldn't get beaten and how Little Sister was forced to watch and that, somehow, I did not think that made for a good childhood and, oh by the way, there are more stories about abuse.

She burst out crying. Said she did not remember doing those things. She was a good Christian woman and would never. And out of the room she went and we never again studied the Bible together.

As time went on and Mother was widowed, she insisted it was only her that ever was abused by her Honey, my Devil. So, is her memory bad, is she delusional, mentally ill, or evil? Maybe she can be all. If so, that's a dangerous combination.

Yet many years later she said she apologized to all my siblings for not protecting them when they were children. I have no way of verifying this because I cannot speak to three of my siblings. Little Baby Brother said he remembered she apologized but wasn't quite sure for what. Still, Mother did not apologize to me. Instead, she slowly drove me around her town running her errands as she made excuses saying, "I'm just weak." Of course this I already knew. Was her admission, or confession, to be her agent of change?

Sadly, it did not prove to be so and my hopes for a genuine love from a mother were dashed once again.

Trust

Good people believe "trust me" implies that to do so will be good for them. Players of confidence games and other evil people know "trust me" is only going to benefit them and that you — the mark, the victim, the prey, the dupe — will not like what happens once they are gone.

So trust is interesting. Smart folks know one can trust that both good and bad things can happen. While there were a few in my life I could trust about good things, there was always that niggling feeling that maybe trust in them was misplaced. In any case, I mostly learned trust was not a good thing.

Yet one cannot go around acting like one suspects everybody of being evil without going nuts. Therefore, I faked trusting. With a smile and a confident handshake, I said I trusted, but if verification was slow in coming, it was time to plan how to get out of or handle the situation. This took a lot of mental energy and kept me in a negative place, both of which kept me drained.

Trust but verify took the calmer form of believing the best of everyone until proved wrong. Once they showed their true colors then BAM!, they were out of my life. This seems to work well and has helped with my other problem.

Hypervigilance

Take a girl with an inquisitive mind, who likes to plan, doesn't like surprises, and who is Big Helper. Naturally she is going to walk into any situation and assess the danger and make a plan of action in case A, B, or C presents itself. Then she will look at the crowd, make threat assessments, judge response types among crowd members, identify all points of ingress and egress of the particular venue she is in, and is quietly so alert that she notices where total strangers are sitting and picks up on all disturbances in the energy of the crowd. Sometimes even walking over to that energy disruptor to disrupt — successfully — the negative energy by bringing in happiness and light and support and understanding and...more things that would take the focus off the negative and onto Angela because, after all, Angela was the Big Martyr Willing To Die For Total Strangers Doncha Know.

And after fulfilling her mission of leaving the disruptor in a positive state, she then goes back to her seat where her husband asks for an explanation and she tells him what he wants to hear even if it is a lie because he really has never understood and gets all upset and she doesn't want any more negativity around her.

And he knows it's a lie she's telling. And she knows he knows.

But he doesn't have the strength to grant him the serenity to accept the things he cannot change, nor the courage to change the things he can, nor the wisdom to know the difference. Frankly, serenity and wisdom are not in her, either, so in this the woman and her husband are a match. Courage and cowardice will be constant themes in her life as a result.

Geez. I was flat worn out. Looking to my Heavenly Father, guess what I found? Why, even He allows people to make their own decisions and live with the consequences. So when the realization hit after all these years that I had not yet run into a *Die Hard* or *Black Sunday* situation wherein I was solely responsible for saving everyone, well then, my ego was shut down.

Yes, prideful ego kept me hypervigilant much longer than I needed to be. Sure, what I did as a child was necessary and I was good at it. Of course there is nothing wrong with planning, being aware of one's surroundings, but when I went into a stadium and had to sit at the highest point with my back against a wall, preferably in a corner where my flanks were protected, and I was having panic attacks after seeing the job was bigger than me but I was the only one...blah, blah, blah, boring, and yawn.

I will say it again: I was flat worn out. Nothing good was happening from my behavior.

The Need to be Remembered

Other than a shared childhood and a weak mother, what else did we siblings have in common? Nothing much. Here was the next ego check, sad to say: Why was it so important to have my family in my life? I could think of but one reason:

I wanted acknowledgement of the sacrifices made for them.

Hell, I needed it. Was trying to get it. Then came the understanding that even Jesus Christ, who died for humans and who said no one has greater love than he who lays down his life for another *(John 15:13)*, and his Father, who allowed His son to go through that horrible death, do not have their sacrifices acknowledged by the majority of humankind. So who am I to demand that same gratitude from just five people I happened to be related to by blood?

Oh, my. That hurt the old ego and I thought: Am I just as sniffingly self-righteous as them? Please, God, if I am, send help to make me see it. And He did. Often. Because, just like Jesus' disciples argued amongst themselves as to who was greatest, it took a while for me to check my ego. Yes...still working on it, too.

God is great.
God is good.

Pretzeling

One way of controlling others was to become what they needed me to be. Acting became second nature until I couldn't tell where I began and the necessary character ended. Someone once told me, "Angela, I never know how you will react. You change constantly." Well, duh. I was hypersensitive to all changes in others and reacted accordingly. Anything to maintain control of the situation so violence would not happen. After all, I was Hypervigilance personified about everybody and everything else except me.

I could not recognize myself in pictures nor pick my voice out of a recording. I often wondered who that person was in a reflection when I walked by. I take a lot of pictures of myself since the divorce. I am the selfie queen. But it isn't because I am so in love with my image. It's simply to remind myself what I look like at any given time. I am often surprised at my image...and not always in a good way.

I change constantly and not on purpose. Some days the pictures are very good and sometimes they are very bad. But I keep them anyway. And I'm having fun with my image, even making fun of myself at my own expense, a thing I would never have thought I could do.

Yet the desire to please, control, and so forth, is still so strong that upon meeting a man I really like, I immediately pick up on his needs and wants and become that thing. It's an automatic response and I hate it. No longer do I feel confident. I second-guess myself. And the man picks up on that. I even had one man say to me, "Now you are just being disingenuous." He thought I was tricking him because the outgoing, confident woman he met and that so intrigued him had changed 180°, leading him to believe I was playing a game.

I was not lying. I was simply not so good at pretzeling myself into yet another believable shape anymore. Somehow I had sussed out what he needed — and was way beyond wrong. Which, honestly, was a good thing for me. Sure, I was upset for a bit, but then I thought "To hell with him. If he cannot live with my imperfections, then he's not the man for me." It was the right call. His comment and my inability meant I was leaving behind these so-called skills, necessary and good for a while, but which had kept me away from the good things that God gave to humans.

I was very comfortable in that place...until I wasn't. No one could have been more surprised about that transformation than me. And so the reconstruction of Angela continued.

The problem with experts is that they already know what they know. For instance, a company has an employee expert in their current systems. But the company is attempting to update and change and improve those systems. Getting rid of old habits and methods and retraining in the new way presents a twofold challenge because...

...experts often take it personally when they are forced to change and next thing you know they are looking for another job.

In essence this is what happened to me. Granted, during my marriage I worked very hard on the negatives ruling my responses and emotions and relationships. But given that the marriage was to a man who was broken and unwilling to work on himself, I was still stalled in the old ways with no hope of getting out of them without taking drastic action. And thus with God's command to "Get out. Get out now!" I was now available for Him to work with me as He chose. How did He choose to teach me?

He sent men to teach me the next thing necessary to work on. Of course, I didn't see a man and say, "Hey, God sent him so he's the One." And while men approached and offered their services all the damn time, which I turned down, there were other men with whom I had completely different experiences. Some lasting a couple of weeks. Some lasting a few minutes. But upon reflecting on that interaction, God's hand in the matter became obvious because with these I learned the next thing to work on.

I always said a prayer after each of these interactions, thanking my Heavenly Father for His care, then got busy on the task He set before me. His methods worked. Pretzeling will always be a natural go-to state because old habits die hard. But, whereas before it would take me years to recognize what I was doing and even longer to address it, now recognition comes in an instant and the addressing of it almost as fast.

There is a passage in the Holy Bible at *1 Corinthians 9:19-22* that goes:

"For, though I am free from all persons, I have made myself the slave to all, that I may gain the most persons. And so to the Jews I became as a Jew, that I might gain Jews; to those under law I became as under law, that I might gain those under law. To those without law I became as without law toward God but under law toward Christ. To the weak I became weak, that I might gain the weak. I have become all things to people of all sorts, that I might by all means save some."

When I started reading the Bible and came across this scripture, I totally understood how to apply it…at least my fourteen-year-old mind did. See? Even the Apostle Paul was like me! He pretzeled himself, too! And so that reaffirmed in my mind that I was on the correct path to sacrifice myself — my very being, my soul, my character, my identity — so that others would be happy.

Talk about misunderstanding His word. Poor ol' God must've been shaking his head at me. Must've been? He was. It's also easy to imagine some deep sighs on his part.

Suffice it to say that I am no longer as worried as I once was about what people think of me. And an interesting thing has happened. I am more flexible in how I interact with folks now. I'm still not comfortable being in crowds; they do drain me. But I'm letting them be them and me be me and isn't that just a much better thing?

Full Circle

My profile for online dating would read:

Creative. Stubborn. Logical. Helpful. Competitive. Romantic. Practical. A loner needful of adoration. Desirous for justice. Hater of bullies. Loves to cook. Loves to dance. Chuckleheads need not apply.

Do you think that would get any takers? Yeah, me neither. But of those things listed above, the two that had the greatest overall impact were "desirous for justice" and "helpful". Which is why I was happy to find out that Almighty God had not left humankind on their own. He had a purpose and that purpose, when it went off-rail, did not change and He knew immediately what was needed to set it all aright. I will not go into all that other than to say true justice will prevail and so I do not get bent out of shape too much when politicians and preachers and other do-gooder activists stir their little pots and beat their little drums and blow their little horns.

Instead, I will point out that the rest of the list, so much in evidence when I was a child, has now reappeared and thus I am getting back to what God intended me to be all along. He understands delay. He understands when it is time to act. And so, He let me know when it was time to get going and I did.

How it came about was this. My spirit had dried and I could no longer generate real enthusiasm for anything. But there I was, faking a smile, still doing what I had always done, feeling God slipping away faster and faster, but praying, praying, praying for guidance. And He gave it, but I was so entrenched in my own — oh, in what was I entrenched? My own wisdom, maybe? — so that when His advice came I said definitively that could not be it. So I got smart, see. And I started giving Him the old fleece test. [To read about the original fleece test, read *Judges 6:36-40*.] If You want me to do that, then make this thing happen. If the other, then make that thing happen.

Oh, I prayed silently, not moving a muscle in my throat or even closing my eyes in case Satan or another demon was watching and would try to fool me with fake answers. In these prayers, it was easy for God to give me the answer I already knew He would approve of. See? I am ever the Big Helper, even to God.

But the answer came back. And not what I expected, either.

I must have misunderstood what He said. So for the next four years I set about doing more fleece tests. Always the answer was the same and never what I expected it to be. Finally, one summer at a big religious convention, surrounded by fifteen thousand fellow worshippers, where I felt lost and alone, I challenged God.

"My dear Father, you know how stubborn I am. You know how dense I can be. You know how I can doubt everything my eyes see and my ears hear when it concerns me. So, listen you, I need you to be more definitive than ever. You. Must. Make. Me. Understand. What. You. Need. Me. To. Do. And you must do it in a way I cannot mistake it. And you must do it right NOW! In Jesus' name I pray, amen."

And no sooner had those words left my brain than the man on the stage turned toward me and said, "Get out. Get out now."

No one else, even the man who spoke, seemed to notice a thing as he went back to his notes and continued with his lesson.

I immediately bowed my head and prayed in thankfulness. Specifically I said, "Oh, You are good." And that is when my journey started to wherever it is God wants me to be. And it has continued apace. Stumbles do happen, but I don't fret nor worry for as long or as hard as I used to because He has His purpose for me. A purpose I do not know, and might not ever, yet seems to be working itself out.

Healing

So the years marched on and I got divorced and I'm praying and I'm working hard to change the shaky parts of my personality and so forth when some family history came my way from a source on Mother's side that shed a brighter light on her. When that information arrived, the question about mental illness was answered. To protect the privacy of the source, who had no idea what that information meant, I am not going to mention whence this information came, but it was impeccable. Again, this knowledge would prove my Heavenly Father sent what I needed when I best needed it.

Within me was the little girl wishing for hugs and approval and smiles from Mama. The more the little girl did not get those, the more she believed she was unlovable. The more she believed she was unlovable, the more she did not know who she was, why she was here, and sought approval from anywhere just to fill those empty places. This did not work out so well in the long run and all my methods weren't working. Then here came the new information. My mother's complete backstory, if you will.

Now I had a broader context upon which to evaluate Mother's actions and attitude toward me, and could more accurately deal with my emotions about her. She was definitely mentally ill. I have not attempted to even guess at which type of mental illness (or illnesses?) because, frankly, it doesn't matter. There is no way of verifying my guess and labeling it won't change anything anyway. But I sure did get some peace in my heart, soul, and mind.

I no longer believe Mother is evil. Evil knows what is wrong and does it anyway. Mother tried very hard but her mental — emotional? — weaknesses only allowed her so much flexibility in approaching life. With the new information, I came to realize she does the best she can with what she has.

Of course, the fallout of her choices on me and my siblings was still just as bad. But the difference between me and Little Baby Brother and the rest of our siblings is that we want to hear the truth. We might be afraid of what we will hear, but we both recognize that light shed on dark places can only help. Yes, Little Baby Brother is coming to better understand that talking about things does not hurt.

Years ago I watched a British movie called *Cold Comfort Farm*. The movie is based on a 1932 comedy novel of the same name. To control her family, the grandmother character manipulated them with a horror only she had seen in her youth. When the family wanted to do something that she didn't like, she'd screw her face up and get loud and anxious and say, "I saw something nasty in the woodshed." Invariably everybody backed away and let her be.

Her grandson, played by Rufus Sewell, was gorgeous. Dumb as a brick, but Lordy did he ever look good on film, which is discovered by an American relative who comes to stay at the farm and next thing you know a Hollywood director is there to sign him up to be In The Movies. Well, that just would not do and Grandma trotted out the famously manipulative line "I saw something nasty in the woodshed." Everybody froze, as was their habit. Everybody except the Hollywood director who shot back at her —

"Yes, but did it see you?"

I laughed and laughed at that. Mother and siblings freeze when the specter of accurate memory arises. I say, "Take the power away from these memories by bringing them in the open." And thus this memoir with the expanded explanation. I grieve for all the energy I've spent for far too long on activity ineffectively employed. But I don't grieve for too long because look what my Heavenly Father has done for me. I would rather honor that which comes from Him than wallow in sorrow.

The old children's gospel song written by Harry Dixon Loes said, "This little light of mine, I'm gonna let it shine." As Jesus said, "You are the light of the world. A city cannot be hid when situated upon a mountain. People light a lamp and set it, not under the measuring basket, but upon the lampstand, and it shines upon all those in the house. Likewise let your light shine before men, that they may see your fine works and give glory to your Father who is in the heavens." *Matthew 5:14-16*

Happy families are a mystery to me. I do not understand them, though I have always attempted to have one. Only partially achieved, I can honestly say. To this day I get antsy when around a "happy" family for too long, preferring solitude. In solitude I don't have to guess at the dynamics and wonder if I trod where angels fear to tread.

Yet I crave the concept. Which brings us to the God-sent healing mentioned before. It came in the form of an aunt on my father's side. (You can see her picture at the front of the book in the group of Kell siblings.)

One year older than my mother, Pearl Naomi Kell Peavy Vonderhaar retired as a full professor and department head with the University System of Georgia. She had a master's degree in English and was beloved by her students. Aunt Pearl was never happier than when she could have a party and feed people. Next-to-youngest of fourteen, she grew up hungry, so food was a big deal and something to be shared when gotten and appreciated when eaten.

She was a well-known and -liked volunteer in several Conyers, Georgia, civic and social organizations. If you wanted something done, Pearl could rattle the bones of lazy volunteers. She was willing to step into the fray and if somebody didn't like her go-get-'em-make-it-happen spirit and attitude, she would say "To hell with them."

She was much loved by her many nieces and nephews who did grow up knowing her. She was quietly helpful to countless folks, not tooting her own horn. Widowed at 48, she thoroughly enjoyed over fifteen years of being fancy free, but then marrying a widower when she turned 65. I did not grow up knowing her, but when my husband and children and I moved, we found she didn't live far from us. So Aunt Pearl and I started having lunch and doing things together every now and then. It was her wisdom that kept me sane — and from being stupid — during and after the divorce.

Everywhere we went people thought she was my mother.

We looked alike.

We were both tall.

We both loved making things happen.

We talked alike.

We had the same sense of humor.

We were both practical with a thick, stubborn romantic streak running at our very cores.

Her color palette was Summer, mine, Winter; we couldn't share clothes without looking sickly, but oh, how we both loved words. Books were her thing. That she had a writer for a niece simply put her over the moon. She was so happy to say, "This is my niece, Angela Kell Durden. She's a writer. Lots of published books."

She fairly beamed. A Kell was a writer!

I ate it up — while at the same time being uncomfortable with the admiration. Again, something we were both alike in.

She was one of the trusted relatives who read *Twinkle* and was able to fill in many holes for me. Thank goodness she got to see it before her memory went. It was through her and her sister, Aunt Virginia, that I finally got to know my father for the good man that he was. They sent me a series of pictures my father took of himself in a photo booth when he was fifteen. He twinkled, too.

So that's where I got my twinkle from. I cried when I saw it.

Pearl never wanted children. She never longed for them like her siblings did. She never missed not having them. Until she was an old woman, that is. Oh, how she loved to see me. Her eyes would light up and I could make her laugh. And she'd tell me some snarky little comment and I would laugh or agree or nod sagely. Aunt Pearl loved my hugs and I loved hers. "What are you working on now?" would be followed by details of this or that project.

Anyway, after seven years of marriage it became very clear Aunt Pearl had Alzheimer's, and her husband, older than she and in worse health and also losing his mind, could not care for her. Adding to the challenges, she had a lifelong menace of insulin-dependent diabetes with a cascading array of other health troubles. She had named me her fallback care person in case her husband was unable. He was unable and I was called upon.

Gladly I took complete control of her life and healthcare with a determination to make the last years she had joyous. No matter how many times I'd say "she's my aunt", staff, nurses, and doctors never failed to ask "How's your mother doing?" I stopped correcting them after a while because, frankly, it felt good to have her as my mother.

I always focused only on the positive with her. She did not like negativity and it badly affected her. In this we were the same, too. One rule for all of her visitors was that they had to make her laugh. Tell funny stories of way back when y'all were young and did that thing or went to that place. Pearl had long-term memories and for some time could add details, even correct their memories.

But, when her friends started getting weepy, I'd stand behind Pearl and shake a finger at them to stop that, then using gestures would indicate to put on a smile and laugh. Some, so concerned for their loss of a friend, couldn't even for a moment make the sacrifice to even pretend to be upbeat. These were hustled out before Pearl had the opportunity to soak in those negative vibes. Vibes that always had an immediate deleterious affect upon her health.

Even as she lost all memory of everyone and everything, she always knew me. Every day I was at the 24-hour memory care facility, once, sometimes twice. Zealously checking all her meds and ensuring proper care. Questioning and confirming. Keeping the staff on their toes — or else. All hours I'd drop by.

If she was in the hospital, so was I, never leaving her side until Cousin Karen stopped by for a little bit allowing me to go home and shower.

Her bit of fun was going out for lunch or for coffee or riding with me to go check mail at the post office. She adored our outings — until the effort became too much for her. Then it was encouraging her to eat enough. Or exercise a bit more. Or helping to clean up her "accidents". Overseeing her wound care. Tricking her with a happy red plastic shot glass full of pudding laced with Vitamin C and acidophilous while she was on antibiotics. Oh, how she loved her pudding cup delivered by her niece. Proud of it, she was.

Until, finally, hard decisions had to be made and, with her doctor, I stood next to her and explained it was now time to make those hard decisions on her behalf following the very explicit orders she had memorialized in a legal document. Decisions she was happy with. Decisions she knew I would make on her behalf no matter the sacrifice to myself.

Then she was gone and I cried for her. But now I could also cry for my loss. So our lives aligned at the right time for us both and, as a result, I no longer miss my mother like I used to and that pain has eased. That I no longer have that sharp pain regarding my mother is a regret, too.

God, my wonderful, loving Heavenly Father, knew I needed a mama upon whom I could pour out all my love and attention. He knew Pearl needed a child to adore her. Aunt Virginia said, "I believe God made it so that you would be available for Pearl."

Our Father provided for us both. In this matter I have no doubt.

I do not know what my Heavenly Father has in store for me. I don't know why His eye has been upon me or how He wants to use me. I don't know what paths He will set me upon nor how He will use me to further His will. But this I do know:

He wants me to continue to twinkle. And so I shall.

Angela Marie Kell Durden
From the sofa in her peaceful home
December 2019

ACKNOWLEDGEMENTS

I am forever indebted to Tom Whitfield. His editing never ceases to amaze me. He has the eye of an eagle and the willingness to allow this writer to break rules if it will help her tell her tale.

Tom is a true friend…no doubt, one sent by my Heavenly Father.

And to Terry Cantwell who made one simple suggestion that made me remember a huge chunk I had forgotten to put in the afterword. Thank you. Your insights have been much appreciated.

And to the Jedwinistas, my writing critique group since 2009: They got first look at the new material. Their feedback proved invaluable. Thank you to Jedwin Smith, Roy Richardson, Sean Hastings, Shane Etter, Jim Butorac, Candis Stephens, Cathy McCabe, and Fred Whitson for allowing this woman to dump emotionally raw material on them and yet they still made sense of it.

angeladurden.com | angeladurden-books.com

contact the author at: angeladurden@gmail.com

9 781950 729036

THIS LITTLE LIGHT OF MINE:
TWINKLE REVISITED
BLUE ROOM BOOKS
DECATUR, GEORGIA
978-1-950729-03-6

Made in the USA
Columbia, SC
21 March 2020

89185164R00135